MW01627180

THAT WILL SAVE YOUR LIFE

THE SEVEN NUMBERS THAT WILL SAVE YOUR LIFE

First Edition

Published by: Rapha Seven, 923 Parkview Lane, Southlake, TX 76092

Unless otherwise noted, italics and bold treatment used in quotes indicate the author's added emphasis.

DESIGNER: Gelson Rocha

Printed in USA

SCOTT CONARD, MD,
DABFM, FAAFP

THAT WILL SAVE YOUR LIFE

www.rapha7ven.com

DEDICATION

This book is dedicated to Pat Dunn, a dear friend and visionary who has clung tightly to his vision of great healthcare and long life for every person. We have been through much together in our quest to find ways to inform and support people who are ready to live long and vital lives. He won the Healthcare Hero award for the Dallas Business Journal in 2008 for his innovation and ingenuity in healthcare. He will always be an inspiration, an admired colleague and a dear friend.

NOTE FROM DR. SCOTT CONARD:

This is the first edition. The only constant in medicine is change and so we hope that in future editions we will be able to report significant improvements and perhaps even curing of many of conditions discussed in this edition.

The commitment of this book is to be as accurate as possible. Feedback and criticism with the intent of improving the content is always welcome and appreciated. Please forward your thoughts to me at **scott@thesevennumbers.com** contents

THE SEVEN NUMBERS

foreword
THE SEVEN NUMBERS

Ignorance is bliss … until it kills us or debilitates us through blindness, amputation, kidney failure, a stroke or a heart attack. Often the process of overcoming our ignorance comes too late, when too much damage has already been done and there is no way to slow or reverse the process. Only then do we discover what we could have done to keep us from our fate.

Growing up on the coast of Florida, I observed the miraculous wonders of nature, both in its splendor and its destructive fury. In a matter of hours, the beautiful, rolling ocean could go from serene to violent, from bringing pleasure to devastation. The human body holds miraculous wonders as well. While it has the potential for tremendous strength and stability, it also holds the potential for weakness and conflict. Our *choices* determine our path. We can be proactive or passive. Either way, we will reap the consequences of our choices. They are unavoidable.

The timeless truth holds true: "…People are destroyed for lack of knowledge… (Hosea 4:6 NKJV). I have served as a physician for nearly twenty-five years and have witnessed firsthand the destruction a lack of knowledge can bring. Irreversible conditions, including going to dialysis three times a week, needing a seeing eye dog, or living life paralyzed in a wheelchair or a nursing home all result when people are uninformed of the consequences of poor lifestyle choices or choose to not act on the knowledge they have.

As disturbing as this may be, my hope is not to scare you, but to motivate you to pursue good health. I have stood by the bedside of too many good people who did not act; and then, when they realized the severity of their situation, it was too late. I am resolved to not let that happen to you. This is why I have developed *The Seven Numbers That Will Save Your Life*. It is written in easy-to-understand, memorable terms, so that you can determine your trouble spots and develop the healthy habits you need to add years to your life and life to your years.

You were created to live an abundant life—one that is healthy, vibrant, and full of purpose. And you don't need a medical degree to do it. By learning how to set and achieve your health goals, you can focus on the important things in life, such as enjoying relationships, developing your talents, having peace in your heart and sharing love and joy with others. From there, it is my desire that you will become an outspoken advocate of good health, sharing what you learn with others so they too can experience the rewards of good health.

As you go through this journey, I encourage you to share your challenges and triumphs with us. Go to **www.thesevennumbers.com** and tell us how these principles are working in your life. Together, we will find the answers and path you need to help you truly succeed.

I look forward to our journey together!

Scott Conard, MD

SECTION ONE
GETTING STARTED

IT'S AS SIMPLE AS A, B, C

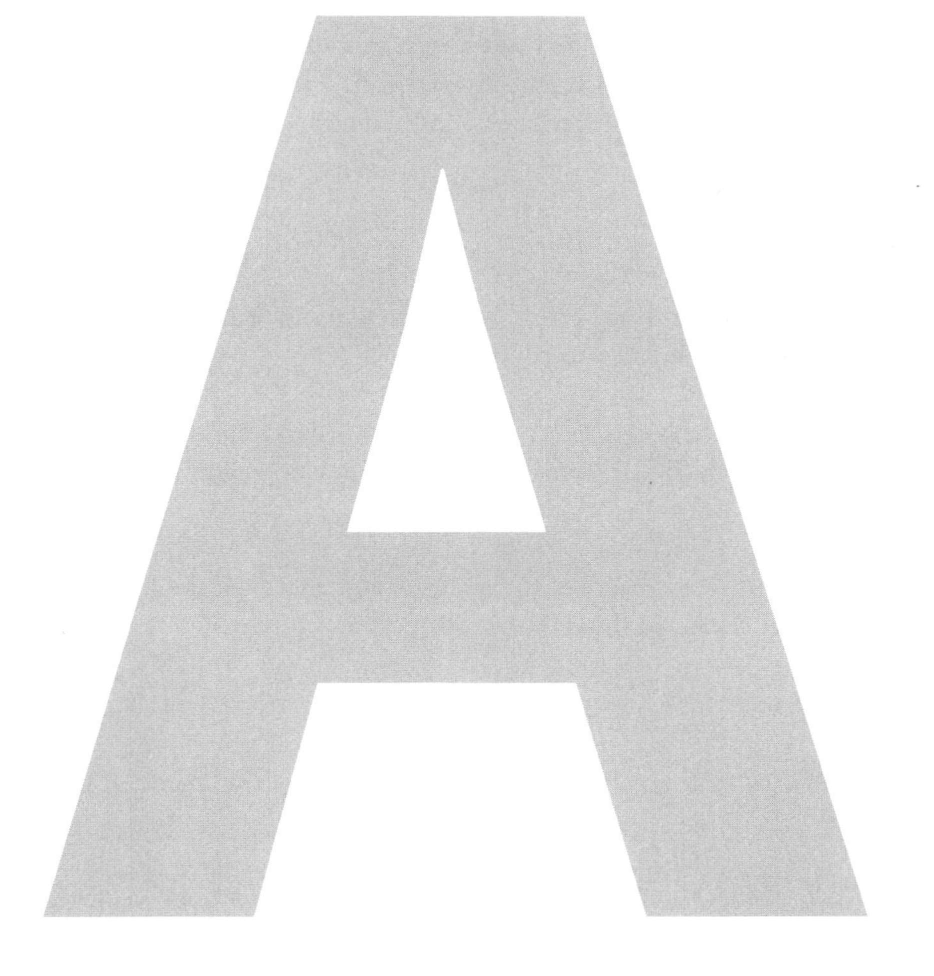

UNDERSTANDING THE SEVEN NUMBERS

The first part of any trip is realizing where you are and deciding where you want to go. Likewise, achieving health and fitness starts with assessing where you are now and where you want to be in the days ahead. To do this, I took the word TROUBLE and developed an acronym that stands for seven primary areas of importance connected with our physical health. In the word TROUBLE…

T is for ***Training***: It shows the amount of activity in your life as reflected in your level of fitness.

R is for ***Roundness***: It can be captured by your waist circumference or your Body Mass Index (BMI), a formula comparing your weight in relation to your height.

O is for ***Oil***: It is a measure of the quantity and quality of the fats in your blood (triglycerides, LDL, HDL).

U is for ***Unacceptable Sugar***: It indicates the sugar levels in your blood.

B is for ***Blood Pressure***: It measures the pressure on the inside of your blood vessels.

L is for ***Lousy Habits***: It identifies things in your life that hold you back from good health.

E is for ***Exploding Plaque***: It exposes the fat buildup inside your arteries that leads to cardiovascular disease (heart attacks and strokes), the #1 killer in the U.S. for both women and men.

By assessing your TROUBLE numbers, you can accurately determine where you are in the spectrum of good health—healthy, borderline, or unhealthy. Let me explain with these three diagrams.

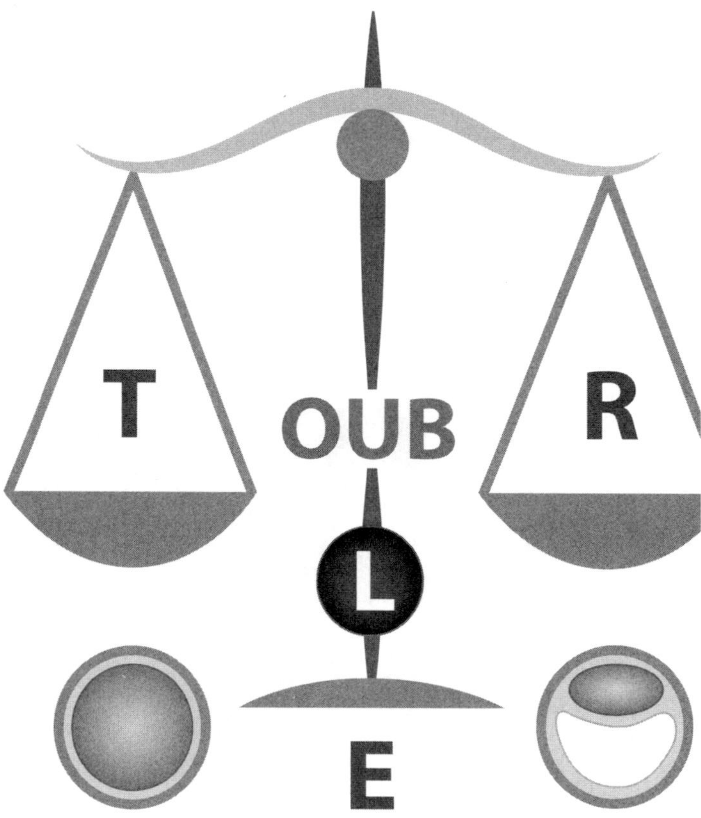

What is shown in this first diagram is that the balance between training (**T**) and roundness (**R**) manifests in our body in how much oil (**O**) and unacceptable sugar (**U**) are in our blood and what our blood pressure (**B**) is. Any lousy habits (**L**) in our lives, such as smoking and tobacco use, will accelerate the process of exploding plaque (**E**) accumulating in the walls of our arteries.

This second diagram reveals the dangers of a decrease in training (**T**) and an increase in roundness (**R**).

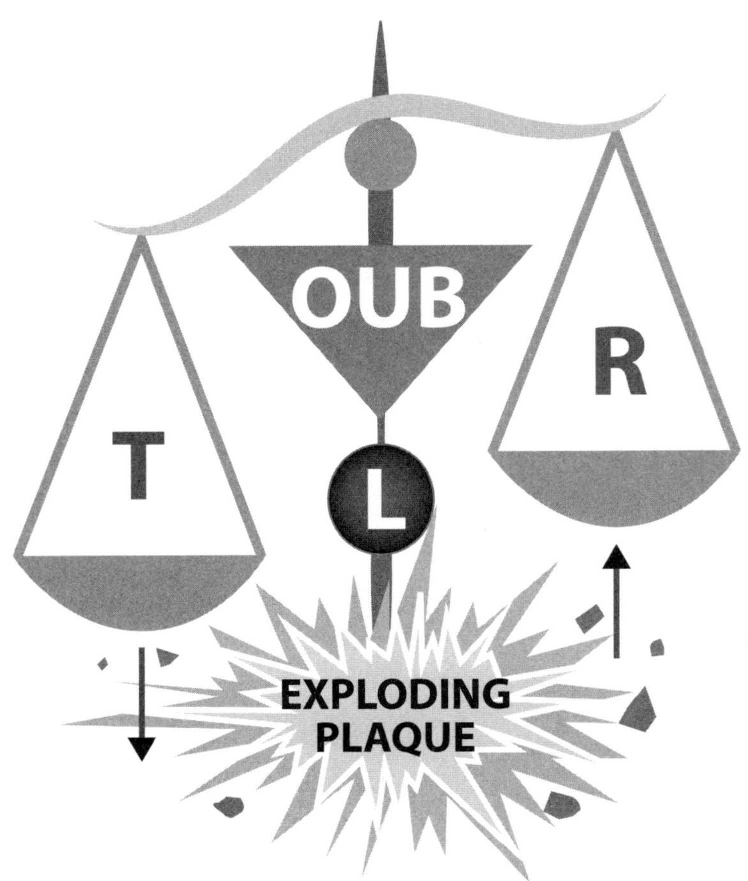

If our training decreases and our food intake remains the same or increases, we are going to have TROUBLE. This is particularly true if we consume an increased amount of saturated or trans fats starchy or refined carbohydrates. When this happens, the amount of unhealthy oil (**O**) and unacceptable sugar (**U**) in our blood increases, and our blood pressure (**B**) rises. Again, lousy habits (**L**) will accelerate this process.

In this third diagram, we see the positive outcome of increased training and the elimination of lousy habits.

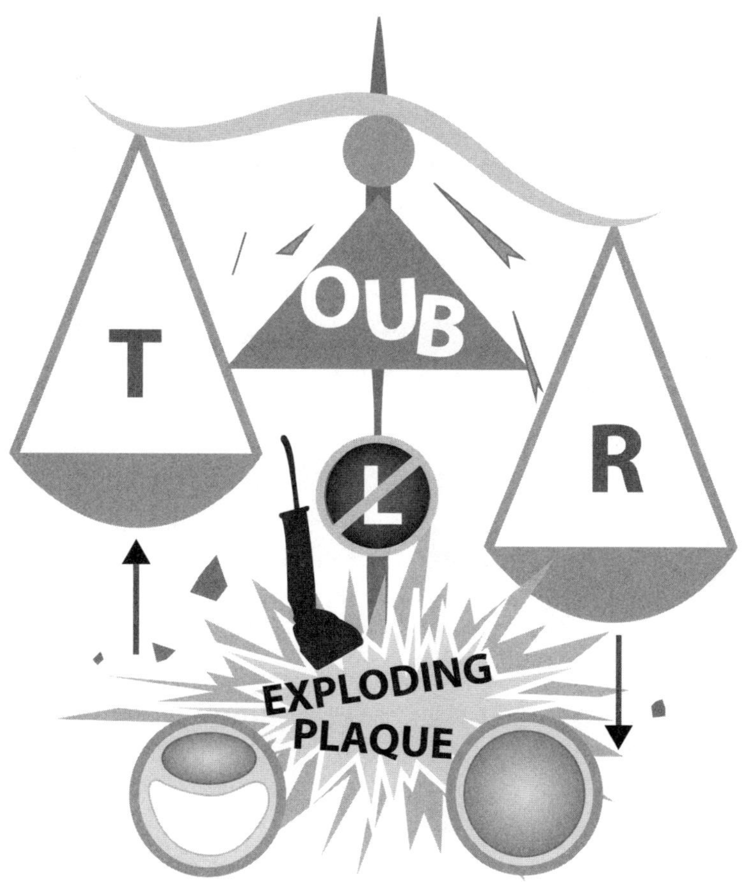

When our training (**T**) *increases*, our roundness (**R**) decreases, and the destructive oils (**O**), unacceptable sugar (**U**), and blood pressure (**B**) also decrease. This reduces the risk of plaque formation and the danger of unstable exploding plaque (**E**) in the walls of our arteries, which reduces the chances of heart disease and stroke.

Improving the quality and length of life, starts with understanding The Seven Numbers. In this book, we will carefully evaluate each of these seven TROUBLE areas and how they interact with each other to determine how well you are doing at your present point in life. We will also define your goals and help you develop a plan of action to achieve them and experience better health.

LEARN YOUR SEVEN NUMBERS

1	**T**	*Training* and fitness
2	**R**	*Roundness* or Body Mass Index (BMI)
3	**O**	*Oil* or fat levels
4	**U**	*Unacceptable Sugar* level
5	**B**	*Blood Pressure*
6	**L**	*Lousy Habits* in your life
7	**E**	*Exploding Plaque* risk within your arteries

PLAYING THE GAME OF HEALTH

Now that you know The Seven Numbers, let's take a look at how they fit into the Game of Health. I call it the Game of Health to make things fun and easy to understand. The game we will compare achieving better health to is baseball—a favorite American pastime you are probably familiar with.

To help us understand the Game of Health, let me introduce "Mary," an example of many of the patients I see. Mary is a thirty-four-year-old mother of three young children who recently divorced and works full-time. She is on the run from 5:00 a.m. to midnight every day. She came to me complaining of headaches, fatigue and upset stomach. She is quite overweight and has type 2 diabetes. Mary is overwhelmed with work, caring for her children and the stress of life. Her diabetes is poorly managed, her blood pressure and cholesterol are dangerously high, and she smokes. Clearly, Mary's health is in serious TROUBLE.

The Game of Health was developed to help patients like Mary make the transition from being *reactive* and having her life "thrown" at her to being *proactive* and having her go after life. Somehow she needed to become aware of her health issues, understand what was causing them, and cultivate some new habits to see things change. That's the essence of the **five steps** in the Game of Health.

STEP 1
AWARENESS

STEP 2
UNDERSTANDING

STEP 3
HABITS

STEP 4
ACCOUNTABILITY

STEP 5
SHARING

5 STEPS TO SUCCESS:

STEP 1 **AWARENESS:** We discover and accept we have a problem.

STEP 2 **UNDERSTANDING:** We learn about the problem and how it works.

STEP 3 **HABITS:** We find out how the habits we have are contributing to the problem and learn new habits to overcome it.

STEP 4 **ACCOUNTABILITY:** We develop a plan of action and tell trusted friends about it, making ourselves accountable to them as we work it out.

STEP 5 **SHARING:** Finally, as we experience success, we share with others what we have and are learning, which deepens our commitment and understanding and propels us to more success.

WE ALL START OUT IN **THE DUGOUT OF LIFE**

We sit back, eating, drinking and watching others play the game. It is a comfortable place. We can yell and cheer and feel like we are in the game, but the truth is we are on the sidelines. No one is looking at us. We aren't attracting attention, and the pressure to perform is minimal. In our minds, we can visualize ourselves at the plate. What stars we would be and what a difference we would make. There's only one problem: Just *thinking* about what we would, could or should do doesn't bring about the solution. It is only when we take action and get in the game that we can win.

AWARENESS IS **GETTING IN THE GAME**

The first thing that Mary and all of us need to do is make the choice to get out of the dugout and step up to the plate. As problems are "pitched" at us, we need to begin taking swings at solving them. This is where healthcare providers come in. Wisdom from doctors, nurse practitioners, physicians' assistants, dietitians, physical therapists, chiroprac-

Changes in our body are the result of a logical series of steps. By discovering these changes, we discover the quality of our health and where we are in the process. Many times when we are dealing with disease, it can be slowed or even prevented once discovered. The key is learning to look and listen to what is going on inside us. For example, the average person who develops type 2 diabetes has had "pre-diabetes," or metabetes, for 5 to 15 years before then. During this window of time, the chance of stopping or reversing this process is possible! Where are you in the process of developing high blood pressure, lipid (fat) abnormalities, diabetes and blood vessel disease?

tors, psychologists and other licensed professionals, help us gain valuable insight and *awareness* about what is going on in our body. At this point it is vital to our success that we receive good information and encouragement. Getting in the Game takes courage!

UNDERSTANDING IS **MAKING IT TO FIRST BASE**

Once we step up to the plate and begin taking swings at our problems, eventually we are going to get a hit. Over time, as we read good books, listen to CD teachings and audio books, speak with our trusted advisors, go to visits at our doctor's office, and apply the principles to our lives, we are going to discover the right answer for the problem we are facing.

Initially, Mary was resistant to taking the time to slow down and learn about her condition. Feeling overwhelmed, she couldn't see how she could spare one more minute in her life. But she realized that she couldn't keep doing the same things and expect to get better results. Over the next several weeks, she gave up her regular TV and radio shows and listened to audio books in the car and as she did her chores at home. She also kept her office visits and began learning how cholesterol, metabetes (metabolic syndrome or pre-diabetes), diabetes, stress, and smoking affected her body. As she swung at her problems with new solutions, she began to connect and make progress.

To help you find solutions that are a hit in your life, we have made a number of resources available to you online. Go to **www.thesevennumbers.com** and print out the materials and watch the videos on the "opponents" that will try to take you out of the game. You can also download and listen to the audio teachings while you drive, exercise or relax. Don't forget to track your progress as you apply new solutions. Through *understanding* we can begin to defeat our problems and make our way to second base!

ROUNDING THE BASES RESULTS FROM DEVELOPING GOOD **HABITS** AND **ACCOUNTABILITY**

Once we have become AWARE of our TROUBLE spots and UNDERSTAND how they work in our lives, we will have successfully arrived at first base. At this point, we must ask ourselves, "What am I doing that is feeding this problem?" Discovering bad HABITS and cultivating good HABITS is one of the things that keeps us rounding the bases. By learning what the problem is and how other people have gotten into TROUBLE, we can more easily see what we need to do to change it. To help you discover these habits, use The Seven Healers Assessment at **www.mysevenhealers.com**.

The other thing that helps us round the bases is having ACCOUNTABILITY. While at first it may look like changing habits will be easy, we will soon discover it is not. We will need the help of trusted friends if we are going to break free from unhealthy patterns. By sharing our plan of action with others and being accountable to them to carry it out, we will experience progress. That is why the Good Book says, "Confess to one another therefore your faults (your slips, your false steps, your offenses, your sins) and pray [also] for one another, that you may be healed and restored [to a spiritual tone of mind and heart]..." (James 5:16 AMP) Healing and restoration comes as we are accountable to others.

*Who you play the game with is really important. In **The Seven Healers** we discover the powerful role others play in helping us win or lose the game.*

So who can you lean on for support? Who will not condone your wrong choices but at the same time not condemn you when you fail? Who encourages you to be active and live healthy? What good habits can you develop to become more active and deal with stress in a healthy way? Healthy relationships and habits are major keys to winning the game of health. Once your environment supports you, instead of undermining you, you can successfully reach third base.

SHARING WHAT YOU'VE LEARNED MEANS YOU'RE **HEADING FOR HOME**

You now officially rock! You have figured it out and have begun to win the Game of Health. There is one step left and that is SHARING your success with others. Begin to teach a friend how you have succeeded, which will allow them to better care for his/her body.

We learn the most from those who are one step ahead of us and one step behind us. Who in your life has a healthy, balanced life that you admire and can learn from? Take some time to get to know them.

When I was a resident physician at Parkland Hospital, we had a saying about how to become a more competent doctor: "See one, do one, teach one." After we saw a procedure performed, we did it ourselves under the proper supervision. Once we could confidently perform the procedure on our own, we taught our co-interns and residents how they could do it. This not only allowed us to serve our fellow interns and residents, but it also forever ingrained the procedure in our minds. That's the power of sharing.

Don't look for some faraway expert to teach your loved ones. Begin to teach them yourself! As you SHARE what you have learned, your life and theirs will begin to change, grow, and succeed in ways you have never imagined.

CONGRATULATIONS!

You have successfully arrived at home plate and won the Game of Health. You became AWARE of the problem, got UNDERSTANDING on how it worked, and figured out what HABITS in your life were "feeding" it. You set new goals and recruited your friends and family to the game to be ACCOUNTABLE and help you win and keep on winning. Now you are SHARING how you won and supporting and mentoring others to become winners too. All five of these steps in the Game of Health will be used at the close of each chapter to help us better grasp and apply the principles of The Seven Numbers.

PUTTING IT ALL TOGETHER

With an overview of The Seven Numbers under our belt and an understanding of how to play the Game of Health, let's take the next step toward better health. Along with the life-changing principles in this book, you must have a *willingness to know and understand* how your body works and a *willingness* to act upon the knowledge you learn. Knowledge without action is like having the most technologically advanced and equipped sports car but no gas to make it go. Therefore, the question is …

ARE YOU IN **A TEACHABLE MOMENT**

I have spent my medical career watching, waiting and even trying to induce *teachable moments* in my patients. As I hear their life story, learn their habits and examine their body, I am often filled with a sense of foreboding about their future. By the end of the visit, I usually have a clear picture of what can be done to reduce the risk of major health problems in their lives. However, if my patient does not see the urgency in their situation and is not willing to take action, he is not in a teachable moment. I could try all day to convince or coerce him to do something, but it would be useless.

The fact that you are reading this book tells me that you are probably in a teachable moment. You may be are tired of not fitting into your clothes, tired of taking lots of pills, or tired of being stuck in the same set of problems. Whatever the case, you are ready to learn and are open to new choices. You are at the crossroad of life where transformation can begin, and that is exciting!

THERE ARE **NO QUICK FIXES**

Although American life revolves around fast food, fast transportation, fast computers, fast corporate changes, get-rich-quick schemes, and quick weight loss diets, there are no fast ways to fix health problems. Overcoming poor health issues is going to take time. It is a process. As Earl Nightingale says, *"Success is the progressive realization of a worthy ideal."* Quick fixes give an illusion of quantum leaps forward—something that will make up for lost time and effort. However, quick fixes act more like quicksand, keeping us stuck right where we are.

Instead of a quick fix, we are going to focus on small steps that bring transformation. Lifestyle changes developed *little by little* bring lasting improvement. This is ageless wisdom. In the Old Testament of the Bible it states; God told the Israelites, "...I will force out your enemies *little by little* and give your nation time to grow strong enough to take over the land" (Exodus 23:30 CEV). In the same way, we are going to learn how our body works and begin to make adjustments little by little until we become strong enough to totally reclaim our health. It is the daily small steps toward our goal and the appreciation of each accomplishment that set the tone and build momentum that produces success.

THIS BOOK CAN **SAVE YOUR LIFE!**

No, there isn't any magic formula or secret code within these pages. This is simply a guidebook to lead you forward in your journey. It is designed to be interactive and enjoyable and is filled with basic principles on how the human body works and what is needed to experience good health. Also provided within these pages are real stories about real people and the wisdom of their victories and defeats. As you read, I believe your vital goals will come into focus, lighting the path to lasting and satisfying success.

There is time to take care of your health! Countless others are doing it and you can too. As you journey through each chapter, you will engage in continual fine-tuning, acquire new habits and develop a network of encouraging relationships. It only takes a few moments a day over months and years to win. Once you complete *The Seven Numbers*, I encourage you to check out *The Seven Healers*, a book that will help you understand the "inputs" in your life and how to achieve even greater success (**www.mysevenhealers.com**). But before we get into The Seven Numbers, there's one more thing I'd like to share ...

A TALE OF **TWO PATIENTS**

"Bob" came to my office for a checkup after his buddy had a heart attack on the golf course. At age forty-four, Bob understood that he too might be susceptible to heart problems. He felt fine at the time and didn't think there was anything wrong, but he wanted to make sure. As we talked about his medical history, the first red flag went up when Bob told me that his father died of a heart attack in his early fifties. We then went through the results of his physical and lab tests, identifying some additional problem areas.

At the beginning of my career, I would have completed my visit with Bob by handing him a prescription for medicine and telling him to eat better and exercise. Instead, I asked him to take a TROUBLE™ Assessment home, complete it, and return in two weeks. He did and discovered a number of other areas where he was at risk. At that point, he was ready to address the problems—he was in a *teachable moment.* So we started by setting some small, achievable goals, most of which involved increasing his level of activity. I also shared some guidelines for eating called the Hand Signals of Health and started him on a vitamin and medication to lower his cholesterol. We then scheduled a follow-up appointment for six weeks later.

When Bob returned, he had experienced some improvement, which was largely due to the cholesterol-reducing medication. But his numbers showed that he was still in danger. The reason for this was that he had not figured out how to increase his physical activity in the midst of his busy schedule. One thing Bob had done in those six weeks was to take a relatively new test called a Calcium Score or Heartogram.™ Just like a mammogram reveals calcium or a mass in the breast, a Heartogram™ reveals what is going on in the heart. It shows any calcium that may have begun to accumulate in the heart arteries—a clear sign that they may be blocked.

Not surprisingly, there was some blockage, and it was more serious than we expected. The test revealed a significant buildup of plaque in one of his main heart arteries. Right away, I sent him to a heart specialist who ordered an outpatient Computer Tomography Arteriogram (CTA) Scan, which is a noninvasive coronary angiogram (it is done without sticking long needles and catheters into an artery). The test confirmed the blockage, and Bob was started on a very aggressive plan to stabilize and reverse his heart disease. This was Bob's wake-up call.

The next time I saw him, he had been able to stick with the original plan we had developed. He was also using the weekly Seven Healers™ Assessment to track his progress (**www.mysevenhealers.com**. Over the next six months, we worked together to tune-up many of his health habits. Little by little, he increased his daily activity, and as a result, he lost 30 pounds and felt much better! His cholesterol returned to normal and his blood pressure decreased. He was so inspired by the positive changes that he sent in two of his friends for a checkup. They too got on a program and began losing weight and dramatically improving the way they felt. Today, all three of them are playing golf together every Thursday, while supporting and encouraging each other to stay on track. They are playing Game of Health and winning!

Another man, whom I will call "Russell," was not so fortunate. Russell was an outstanding family doctor I had worked with when I was a resident physician. He was my mentor and the father of four very talented children. He was active in his medical group, the community, and our state professional association. He looked and felt strong and healthy. Most of his numbers were excellent. What I didn't know was that he had high cholesterol and a family history of heart disease.

In May of 1996, Russell went out for a jog and never returned. He experienced a major heart attack and was found dead on the side of the road. Hundreds of people, including his family, were stunned and devastated at his loss. A star had been taken from us without any apparent warning.

At that time, the Heartogram™ was not readily available to reveal a buildup of calcium in his heart. Consequently, there was no easy way to look and see if he had heart disease. All he had to draw from were blood tests, which don't always tell us what is going on in the heart. Speaking with his family after the tragedy, I learned that he had begun jogging again and had taken cholesterol medicine off and on. However, because he was feeling good, he often missed doses. The lack of knowledge of his true condition and lack of symptoms gave Russell a false sense of security that I have come to call the lethal "I feel fine" disease, and it proved disastrous. Now I ask you, which scenario will you follow? Either of these people could be you—feeling fine, living life on "cruise control," possibly not realizing you are a time bomb ready to explode (this occurs a few years later in women but is the #1 cause of death. Thankfully, with a greater understanding of how these problems occur, we can find out if you are in TROUBLE and where. All you need to do is …

COMPLETE **THE TROUBLE ASSESSMENT**

Simply go to **www.thesevennumbers.com** and fill out the requested information. In order to complete the assessment, you will need your …

1. **Weight and height**
2. **LDL, HDL, and triglyceride cholesterol values**
3. **Fasting blood sugar level**
4. **Blood pressure**
5. **And an idea of how active you are, measured by a pedometer as steps per day or by the number of minutes you exercise per week.**

Once you have completed the **TROUBLE™ Assessment**, you will have a good idea of the state of your health. You'll know which areas are healthy and which areas have a problem. With this valuable information, you are ready to move into Section II and learn an in-depth overview of each of The Seven Numbers. If there are chapters that don't seem applicable to you, feel free to skim through them.

Time is of the essence. Once you know where you have issues, you are closer to averting disaster and restoring health than you think. And the best time to begin fixing the problem is now! So take a few minutes and fill out the TROUBLE™ Assessment at **www.thesevennumbers.com**.

Again, if you have any questions, concerns, or want to share your challenges or victories, I would love to hear from you. You can contact me at **www.thesevennumbers.com**. Thank you in advance for your input. Now let's take a deep breath and head into *Training*.

SECTION TWO
THE SEVEN NUMBERS
IDENTIFYING AND ADDRESSING YOUR TROUBLE SPOTS

NUMBER ONE

"Nothing turns back the clock faster than a consistent regimen of exercise. Sure, aging is inevitable, and yes, Scripture tells us that 'it is appointed for men to die once' (Hebrews 9:27 NKJV). But those facts don't give us license to shuffle into old age, looking for a park bench to sit on. I believe we should exercise because God designed our bodies like finely tuned cars; if we never leave the garage, our batteries die. If we put our bodies through the paces, we add years to our lives—productive years that can be used in ministry or add value to the lives of others."

Jordan Rubin

Jordan Rubin, *The Great Physician's Rx for Health and Wellness* (Nashville TN: Thomas Nelson, Inc., 2005) p. 136.

TRAINING

The **T** in our TROUBLE Assessment stands for Training. It is the measure of activity we do on a regular basis and the first of The Seven Numbers that will save your life. Training includes all forms of exercise as well as physical activity. Clearly, our bodies were made to move.

Over the past several decades, the overall amount of training of Americans has decreased dramatically. With the dawn of the industrial age of the twentieth century, major changes were well underway that would result in dramatic differences in the amount of daily activity people participated in.

LIVING A **SEDENTARY LIFE**

As the industrial age brought about a greater specialization of duties, the percentage of the population involved in manual labor, particularly farming, decreased. Less manual labor meant a less active population. As a result, the amount of energy, or food, needed by these individuals also declined. Additionally, as people gained access to new luxuries, such as cars, refrigerators, electricity, and standard plumbing, the activity level declined even more and a sedentary lifestyle set in.

Think about it. With the invention of trains, planes, and automobiles, travel increased but physical activity decreased. Instead of walking or riding bikes to get somewhere, we just hop on whatever mode of transportation is available. With just about every modern-day convenience, we have accelerated the external processes around us but slowed the internal processes within us. Without regular movement, our bodies become stagnant and a breeding ground for problems.

*The **T** in our TROUBLE Assessment stands for Training. It is the measure of activity we do on a regular basis or the level of fitness you possess assessed by a fitness test. Training includes all forms of exercise as well as physical activity. Clearly, our bodies were made to move.*

THE INVENTION OF **FAST FOOD**

Along with the increased sedentary lifestyle came the advent of fast food, causing the opportunities for TROUBLE to exponentially grow. Experts believe that the average amount of food consumed by individuals living in the early days of the industrial revolution initially *declined*, but it wasn't long before this changed.

Food science quickly caught up with the changing lifestyle of Americans. With the invention of refrigeration and improvements in preservatives and packaging, foods could now be stored longer and transported farther than before. This helped the fast food industry make its way to the dinner table in the 1950s. The first of the chain restaurants to pop up was McDonalds, making its grand entrance into society in 1952. Pizza Hut followed in 1958, followed by Kentucky Fried Chicken in 1959.

This trend has accelerated to the point that we now have over 200 different fast food chains encouraging us to stop by and "have it our way." They have made high-calorie food easily available with minimal effort. Sure, it's convenient, but convenience has a price. A regular diet of calorie-dense foods like these is costly to our health and quality of life.

In addition to the proliferation of fast food is the increased amount of processed foods. Currently, food processing is so advanced that we can buy almost any food we want at any grocery store we go to. It's available in a can, in a box, or frozen. The more processed a food is, the less life-giving nutrients it contains. The transition from regularly consuming water, milk, fresh fruits and vegetables, wild game, fish, whole grain breads and rice to processed food has been dramatic.

*The industrial age has led to a **decrease** in physical activity and an **increase** in consumption. Food science has advanced to the point that high-calorie foods are readily available to us at any time. Sure, it is convenient, but this convenience is costly.*

THE INNOVATION OF **ADVANCED TECHNOLOGY**

Another major cause for a decrease in activity over the years is the development of new technology. In the 1950s, television began to find a permanent position in the American home, followed by numerous other inventions and services like VCRs, cable television, microwaves, personal computers, cell phones, the Internet, text messaging, MP3 players, and iPods. Add in a slew of video game gadgets like Atari, Nintendo Play Stations, Game Boys, and Xbox and it is easy to see how our activity level has also continued to decline.

Advanced technology has produced a "lifestyle revolution" over the past decades, and everyone has been affected to some degree. In fact, as we entered the 21st century, we super-sized our bodies to such an extent that America has become a top three contender for the most overweight and obese civilization to inhabit the earth. This is amazing, given the fact that the United Nations estimates over 40,000 people on the planet, mainly children, starve each day. This leads to one conclusion: If we are going to remain healthy, it will be by ***choice***, not default. We must develop a plan to become active and stick to it.

OUR BODY NEEDS **MOVEMENT AND MAINTENANCE**

In some ways, our body is a lot like a car. In order for it to run well, we need to give it regular maintenance. We must keep the tank filled with good gas, change the oil regularly, lubricate the joints, maintain proper air pressure in the tires, and periodically check under the hood. If we drove our car 10 miles per hour for 10 to 15 years, and we gradually added 700 pounds of bricks to the trunk, which is roughly 30 percent of its overall weight, how do you think it would it run? And if we didn't do any maintenance on it until it broke down, what do you think we could expect? That's right. The car would become run-down and soon it would not work. The shocks would be shot, and the oil and fuel lines would become filled with sludge from lack of use and maintenance.

Similarly, our body needs regular maintenance and movement to remain in top working condition. Maintenance includes providing our body with good fuel in the form of good foods and good oil. Appropriate additives, such as fish oil does wonderful things for our health. They strengthen our cells and improve the wear and tear on our joints (suspension). When we exercise and get our engine up to higher speeds, we keep the fuel lines of our arteries from gumming up with exploding plaque. Regular training activates special cells in our muscles that suck up excess energy in the form of fat and sugar from the blood. Long-term training can actually decrease blockages in arteries and reverse the curse that leads to heart disease and stroke.

"Exercise is the best medicine for the body." —*Scott Conard, M.D.*

IT'S TIME TO TAKE **STEP IN THE RIGHT DIRECTION**

By now, you may be thinking, okay, I see the value of training. But how do I get started? The first step in the right direction is to get a *pedometer*. A pedometer is a great little device that measures how many steps a person takes in a day. They cost just a few dollars and easily clip to a person's belt or waistband. At our practice, we ask our patients to wear a pedometer from the time they get up in the morning until they go to bed. They then write down their number of steps each day so we can accurately track where they are in their level of activity.

Before we had the modern conveniences of cars, buses, or other forms of transportation, people walked everywhere, giving them an ample amount of physical activity. This is still the case for the majority of people living in third-world countries and in parts of Europe. It is estimated that the average European takes about 10,000 to 12,000 steps per day. On a recent mission trip to Africa, a group of twenty-one doctors and nurses worked at a clinic in Rwanda. Each of us averaged 15,000 to 18,000 steps a day. Unfortunately, the average American only takes about 1,600 to 3,000 steps a day. Wearing a pedometer will help you determine if you fall into this category.

It is not unusual for a caterer or courier to take over 30,000 steps a day. And an average marathon runner takes over 50,000 steps in about four and a half hours! People who are on their feet for a living are definitely high steppers.

Once you have your pedometer in place, it's time to start increasing your number of steps. The first goal we usually set for our patients is to move from 3,000 steps a day to 6,000. This is the break-even point. Taking 6,000 steps a day is just about 3 miles. At this point you are burning about the same number of calories you are taking in if you are eating an average diet. The next goal is to increase from 6,000 steps a day to 10,000. At 10,000 steps you are walking about 5 miles and are actually burning more calories than you are taking in. If you are intent on losing weight, this is the level you want to be at.

Many patients don't want to guess the number of steps they take in a mile, so we suggest they find a treadmill or walking track where they can accurately measure a mile. Generally, women take an average of 2,000 steps per mile and men 1,700 steps per mile. This number can be used in exchange for the number of steps to see how many calories are burned. Calories are energy units that measure the amount of energy in the food we eat. When a person walks a mile at a leisurely pace, they usually burn about 150 calories. This will be important as we go through the next several chapters and talk about the number of calories in the different foods that we eat.

Now, if you are already in pretty good shape, you may want to measure your activity by the number of minutes you exercise each week instead of the number of steps you take daily. If you are jogging, working out with weights, doing yoga or Pilates, or training for triathlons or marathons, the duration and intensity of your activity is going to equate to a different amount of calories burned. See Appendix A for the Center for Disease Control's recommended exercises and the amount of calories they expend.

At some point on your Training journey, you may want to know how you are doing in relation to others on the same path. For additional tests that you can do to assess your fitness, go to **www.thesevennumbers.com** and learn about additional ways to check your level of training.

WAYS TO INCREASE YOUR STEPS

Park farther away
Walk short distances instead of driving
Take the stairs if you are going up 1 or 2 levels
Walk the mall or a trail nearby
Do more chores like gardening and cleaning
Join a health club
Exercise with a friend weekly

THERE ARE MANY GREAT **BENEFITS OF TRAINING**

When Training goes up, Roundness comes down. And that's not the only thing that decreases. Increased Training reduces Oil (cholesterol), Unacceptable Sugar, and Blood Pressure. Although weight loss does occur, the greatest benefit patients report is an increased level of energy and a general feeling of well-being. Some people are even able to gradually get off of their antidepressants, like Prozac, Paxil, Cymbalta, Prestiq, Zoloft or Celexa. While not all patients can get off these drugs, all do see marked improvement in their overall quality of life.

In addition to feeling better is the benefit of a longer life. While at the Cooper Aerobics Center in Dallas, Texas, Dr. Steve Blair studied the effects of exercise on over 25,000 obese men and 8,000 obese women. He discovered that walking for 30 minutes a day at a moderate pace of 3-4 mph resulted in better fitness and a *longer life*. In another study, Dr. Blair looked at the longevity of four groups of people: thin and fit, thin and out-of-shape, obese and fit, and obese and out-of- shape. Who lived the longest? Yep, the fit and thin. Those who lived the shortest were the obese and out-of-shape. Surprisingly, the group that did the second best was the *obese and fit*, not the thin and out-of-shape. So, if the choice is to remain heavy and be fit or lose weight and become thin, go for heavy and fit. Research suggests that you will live longer.

How about genetics? Do they influence health more than lifestyle? Not necessarily. A study of the Pima Indians living in Arizona who became separated from their relatives in Mexico reveals that lifestyle choices can have a much greater impact on health than genetics. Mexican Pimas who worked hard over *forty* hours a week had a dramatically lower incidence of diabetes and a lower BMI than the Arizona Pimas who only worked hard about *three* hours a week. There is simply no substitute for physical activity when it comes to maintaining good health. Other benefits of regular Training include an improved quality of sleep, less lethargy and

GENES vs. LIFESTYLE

	Arizona Pimas	Mexican Pimas
Height	164	160
BMI	33.4	24.9
Hours of hard work per week	3	>40
% Diabetic, male	54%	6.3%
% Diabetic, female	37%	10.5%

fatigue during the day, more positive outlook on life, less constipation and better digestion, decreased appetite, better food choices, and a decrease in muscle aches and pains after a period of reconditioning. All the effects of increased activity add up. Small increases result in great benefits. In short, we gain a new lease on life when we start to use our body regularly. Now you can see why we say *exercise is the best medicine for the body!*

DEVELOP **YOUR OWN EXERCISE PROGRAM**

Training is a very doable thing for any person of any age. The key is to find activities that are fun and get you moving. As you develop your own exercise program, ease into it. Don't overexert yourself or push too hard too quickly. Take your time and experiment with different things. Here are a few things to consider.

An ideal exercise program packs the greatest benefits when it includes at least three aspects: aerobics, strength training (including core building activities), and stretching. *Aerobics* are brisk, physical activities that get you breathing. They require the heart and lungs to work harder to meet the body's demand for increased oxygen and promote the circulation of oxygen through the blood.[1]

Strength training uses methods of resistance to strengthen our muscles and bones. It includes exercises using weight machines or free weights as well as push-ups and pull-ups. Strength training places pressure on the muscles, causing them to tighten and contract, drawing in energy from the blood to increase their size and power. The effects of cleaning the blood of excess sugar and fat will continue for twenty-four to forty-eight hours after a workout, depending on its intensity. The increase in muscle that results not only provides exterior benefits to our appearance, but also helps give the support our body needs to function internally.[2]

Lastly is stretching. These exercises place particular parts of the body in a position that will lengthen, or elongate, the muscles and associated soft tissues.

---

1 Medicinenet.com.

2. Livestrong.com http://www.livestrong.com/article/336536-strengthening-exercise-vs-cardio-exercise/.

Upon undertaking a regular stretching program, a number of changes begin to occur within the body and specifically within the muscles themselves. Other tissues that begin to adapt to the stretching process include the fascia, tendons, ligaments, skin and scar tissue.[3]

To reap the benefits of aerobics, strength training and stretching, yoga and/or Pilates are strongly recommended as they provide all three aspects concurrently. For more ideas on Training, check out our resources online at **www.thesevennumbers.com**. As you get into the game and begin experimenting with different exercises, the program that is right for you will develop. So increase your Training and watch the TROUBLE spots in your life begin to fade.

TRAINING: PRESSING TOWARD THE GOAL

POOR	IMPROVING	ACHIEVING EXCELLENCE
Less than 30 minutes/ week	45 to 150 minutes/ week	Over 150 minutes/ week
Less than 6,000 steps daily	6,000 to 10,000 steps daily	Over 10,000 steps daily

3 http://www.thestretchinghandbook.com/archives/stretching.php.

PLAYING THE GAME OF HEALTH

5 STEPS TO MAKING TRAINING YOUR OWN

AWARENESS: Are you doing any Training? If so, how much do you do weekly? How about daily? Can you see how your life will improve when you incorporate more Training activities? Where are you in your fitness journey? (Go to **www.thesevennumbers.com** for a free assessment tool).

UNDERSTANDING: Do you understand how a lack of Training leads to major health problems? Which problems caught your attention most? Why? What benefits of Training would you like to experience more in your life? How are you going to start taking more responsibility for your health? What do you need to abandon to lead a healthier lifestyle?

HABITS: What habits are keeping you from participating in Training activities? Is there anything you can do while you are walking or working out that will not add more to your day but rather allow you to be more efficient? List three steps you can take to get into the Training game and become more active (i.e. get a pedometer, park your car further away from the door, or take the stairs).

ACCOUNTABILITY: Who else do you know who wants to get more active? How can you encourage and support each other? Is there a group you can join nearby, such as an exercise class, in which you can be assigned a partner and receive the benefits of mutual encouragement and support?

SHARING: Start a journal or download a free program for your computer or hand-held device. Go to **www.thesevennumbers.com** to record your journey in the game of health. Write down things you learn about health and yourself. Also, how can you be active in a way that is a model for those you care about? What about walking with your child or grandchild? The next walk may be the one they always remember and that changes their life. Remember: See one. Do one. Teach one...

NUMBER TWO

"Dieting is not the answer to keeping weight down. As you have heard many times, almost all people who diet to lose weight regain it (and more). Instead, you need to change long-term patterns of eating and physical activity. Hunger management is key. New patterns of eating must satisfy both physical hunger and the need for sensory pleasure from food."

Andrew Weil, M.D.

Andrew Weil, M.D., *Eating Well for Optimum Health* (New York, NY: Knopf, Borzoi Books 2000) p. 185.

ROUNDNESS

The **R** in our TROUBLE Assessment stands for *Roundness*. It is the measure of your weight in relation to your height—your Body Mass Index (BMI). Roundness is directly linked to Training. When our Training goes up, our Roundness goes down and with this decrease comes a decrease in our level of Oil, Unacceptable Sugar, Blood Pressure, and Exploding Plaque.

Unfortunately, just the opposite seems to be taking place in America. Roundness is on its way up. The acceleration of our portliness really hit full stride in the last ten years of the 20th century. In 1991, only four states had a population of 15 percent or more who were over 30 pounds overweight. By 1999, all but a few states had reached this mark in obesity. Indeed, we have a serious epidemic on our hands.

Sometimes it takes broadening our perspective (no pun intended) to really comprehend the condition we are in. Years ago, my wife and I took our children on a summer vacation to Paris, France. At that time, our twins were six years old and we also had a nine-year-old and a fourteen-year-old. The first thing they noticed was the apparent lack of "normal sized" people. One of our twins actually asked why all the people at the airport were "poor." He thought they couldn't afford food and that was why everyone had a thin to medium build.

We continued our study of the people, plopping down on a bench and trying to guess from which country each person had come. It actually turned out to be quite entertaining. We looked at both how they dressed and their size and then guessed their country of origin. We then examined their bags to see if they had a flag or other identifying mark. The easiest people to spot were the Americans because they were about twice the size of those from other countries. Every so often a group of Americans bounced by, and my kids would say, "American tour," and then giggle hysterically.

Our epidemic of obesity was also confirmed when I attended a recent Texas Rangers game. It was the perfect place to take pictures for my Game of Health presentation. I took over 150 photos, and most of them were of people in the 250 to 400 pound range. It saddened me to realize that there were thousands of morbidly obese individuals at that baseball game. On the way home, I asked my friends who were with me if they noticed the surprising number of obese people. Sadly, none of them had. We have become conditioned to accept obesity as normal in America.

You may wonder why I care so much if we Americans are obese. After all, what business is it of mine? To me it's not a matter of shame, guilt, or anger; it is a matter of life or death. I know the hardships these individuals will face and the pain they and their families will endure if they remain in the condition they are in for years or decades to come. That is why I care.

So what is the solution? How can we wrap our arms around the problem and begin to stem the tide of obesity in our lives? I believe the solution starts with knowing our BMI and how it affects the functioning of our body. Next, we must learn the Hand Signals of Health and begin to put them into practice at every meal. With this understanding and by establishing new habits, we can discover a healthier, longer life.

Obesity has become an epidemic in the U.S. We have become conditioned to accept obesity as normal. An understanding of your BMI and of the Hand Signals of Health will help stem the problem of obesity.

UNDERSTANDING **YOUR BASAL METABOLIC RATE (BMR)**

As I said at the open, *Roundness* is the measure of our weight in relation to our height. This is what is known as a person's Body Mass Index (BMI). Roundness is directly linked to Training. When our Training goes up, our Roundness goes down. Another important principle to understand is our **Basal Metabolic Rate** (BMR). This is the rate at which our body uses or *burns* energy in the forms of fat and sugar to keep us alive and functioning.

Interestingly, if you lie in bed all day and do not move a muscle, your body will still burn a fair amount of energy. The more muscle mass you have, the more energy your body burns. From our experience, we have discovered that the average man's BMR is around 2,000 calories per day, and the average woman's is around 1,400. This means a person *at complete rest* could eat this amount of calories and *not* store any extra energy in the form of fat or sugar (carbohydrates). If he or she remained inactive and began to eat more calories than his or her BMR, those extra calories would be stored in the liver as glycogen or in our fat cells as fat (adiposity). This translates to increased inches.

Maintaining a balance between calorie intake and calories burned is our goal. Unfortunately, many people are out of balance in this area, and as Billy Graham has said, "We are digging our graves with our teeth." Let's take a quick look at the digestive process and find out what happens to our food once we eat it.

Your basal metabolic rate (BMR) is the rate at which your body burns calories in order to function. You could lie in bed all day, not moving your body, and still burn calories. The more muscle mass you have, the more energy your body burns. On average, men burn roughly 2,000 calories/day, and women burn about 1,400.

UNDERSTANDING **THE DIGESTION PROCESS**

When we eat, the first thing we do is break down food in our mouth by chewing. When we swallow, we send ground-up food to our stomach where it is further digested by gastric acids. The digested food then moves into the small intestines where it is broken down into its smallest forms: amino acids (proteins), sugars (carbohydrates), and cholesterol and glycerols (fats). This is accomplished by enzymes released by the pancreas. These macro, or main, nutrients then pass through the wall of the small intestine and into the bloodstream.

They then go up the portal vein, which is near the pancreas, and head toward the liver and then travel to the rest of the body. As the nutrient-rich blood from the gut passes by the pancreas, hormones like insulin are released into the blood stream. They run ahead of the food to notify the organs and every cell of the body to take the nutrients out of the blood. For a more amusing illustration of this process, go to **www.thesevennumbers.com** and watch the video *Follow the Food.*

Each cell in our body is empowered to carry out its daily activities by pulling nutrients from the blood. These nutrients include oxygen, water, energy in the form of fat and/or sugar, and amino acids, which are the building blocks of all cells. They then dump the by-products, or wastes, from their work back into the blood for removal from the body. This includes things such as acids and carbon dioxide.

If the amount of energy brought into our body *exceeds* what is burned, our fat cells take up the excess and store it for future use. Our liver takes excess carbohydrates and sugar (glucose) and converts it into glycogen (2 glucose molecules) or fat (triglycerides). It then sends the fats back into the blood to be transported to the fat cells for storage. We'll go into greater detail on this in the next chapter. This protects the body from adverse effects. Fat cells store energy for the next "famine" or food shortage the body experiences. Fat is also stored in the liver, muscles, skin, tissues of the neck and upper airways, and other organs. The degree to which your body is called on to perform these functions roughly corresponds to your BMI.

ROUNDNESS AFFECTS **OUR ABILITY TO PROCESS ENERGY**

What happened to us on our trip back from Red River is a good picture of what happens inside our body when we take in excess energy and have no room for it. When we have more fat and sugar than our body needs and all our storage places are full, our body scrambles to make room for it. In the process, our cells become overstuffed and very uncomfortable and stressed-out. This leads to a process called inflammation, which we will address more in the section on Exploding Plaque.

BMI of 19 to 24	**fat cells take excess energy out of the blood and store it. They then release it during an active period**
BMI of 25 to 27	**fat cells are more congested and less receptive to insulin's promptings to remove excess energy from the blood**
BMI of 27	**the pancreas has to send out extra insulin, causing it to work overtime**
BMI of 30	**fat cells are resistant to taking in anymore energy. This stage quickly evolves from insulin resistance to pancreatic failure - a condition we call metabetes**

At a Body Mass Index **(BMI) of 19 to 24**, our fat cells willingly take up excess energy when we eat. They then release it back into the bloodstream during an active period when our body needs it.

When we have a **BMI of 25 to 27**, things begin to change. At this point our fat cells are starting to become mildly congested and cantankerous. Depending on how much food we have ingested at a given meal, our fat cells may become less receptive to the extra energy they have to store. The more overloaded they become, the more resistant they are to the messenger hormone *insulin*, which is trying to get them to take the extra energy out of the blood.

Once our **BMI reaches 27**, the problem becomes even more pronounced. This stage is known as early metabetes. Once the pancreas sees extra energy in the form of fat and sugar coming into the body, it begins to produce additional insulin molecules to tell the fat cells to get it out of the blood and store it. Unfortunately, our fat cells are weighed down and not as responsive to insulin's promptings. As a result, the pancreas has to work overtime to make additional insulin to push the fat cells even harder to do their jobs.

Finally, at a **BMI of 30** the fat cells have had it. Even though there are numerous insulin signals floating around in the blood, the fat cells will not respond. They refuse to take in anymore energy. This stage is known as full-blown *metabetes*—the internal, stressful condition just before diabetes. It is at this point that an irreversible change occurs. Since fat cells cannot get bigger, they must *multiply*.

WHAT HAPPENS **WHEN ENERGY EXCEEDS OUR BODY'S NEEDS?**

When a person continues to force food into their system even after they are full, unruly fat cells are forced to accommodate excess energy by stretching as much as they can. When they can take it no longer, they are driven to reproduce themselves. This is similar to what we had to do on our trip home from Red River. We had too much stuff for our vehicle, so the only thing we could do was to increase our storage capacity by adding additional space on the roof. But more room does not necessarily equal a smoother trip.

At some point between the ages of eighteen months and four years old, scientists believe we have developed all of the fat cells we will need for the rest of our life. So, the only way for the body to create more space for excess energy is to create more fat cells. This is *not* a normal process, and it only occurs with a lot of tension and infighting between the fat cells and pancreas. Although additional fat cells can be shrunk down significantly after they are created, they cannot be removed even if weight loss occurs. The only method of removal is surgery.

In the meantime, as our body's tissues are bathed in high levels of insulin, they become increasingly insensitive. This condition is called *insulin resistance syndrome* (IRS). This makes the pancreas work harder and longer hours, which I will explain in more detail later. In many people the pancreas gradually burns out and metabetes turns into *diabetes*—a dangerous condition we will talk more about in the section on Unacceptable Sugar.

What else happens when the energy we take in exceeds our body's needs? At some point the body gets the bright idea to begin storing some fat in the blood vessel walls. It is possible that this too is driven by high insulin levels in the bloodstream. In any case, this key event starts the accumulation of a substance we call "plaque" in the arteries. Plaque buildup is responsible for the majority of heart attacks and strokes, which we will see as we continue our journey.

Another side effect of saturated fat cells reproducing is the additional stress of weight gain. Like the car with 700 pounds of bricks in its trunk, our body begins to ache under the added weight. Our muscles have to propel the additional mass through everyday activities. This causes additional wear and tear on our joints, leading to accelerated arthritis and/or low back pain. The tissues of the neck and throat also begin to fill up with fat, which often collapses the windpipe during sleeping and cuts off the airflow to the lungs. This common condition is known as sleep apnea.

Additional weight gain also stresses the heart. More weight means more tissue to have to pump blood to, which causes our blood pressure to rise. To compensate for this, blood vessels reinforce themselves with a fibrous matrix, becoming stiffer and more inflexible. This serves to worsen the high blood pressure problem and can ultimately lead to heart failure if not dealt with.

The bottom line is: When we continue to feed our body more energy than it needs, we inadvertently set ourselves up to fail. We pit one tissue against another, causing both to struggle to function normally. They end up compromising in order to survive. After a number of years of this internal battle, disease enters the body—or even worse, premature death. Poor health choices rob people of the joy and fulfillment that they have spent most of their lives working for. If you find yourself in this position, it's time to wake up and make some changes.

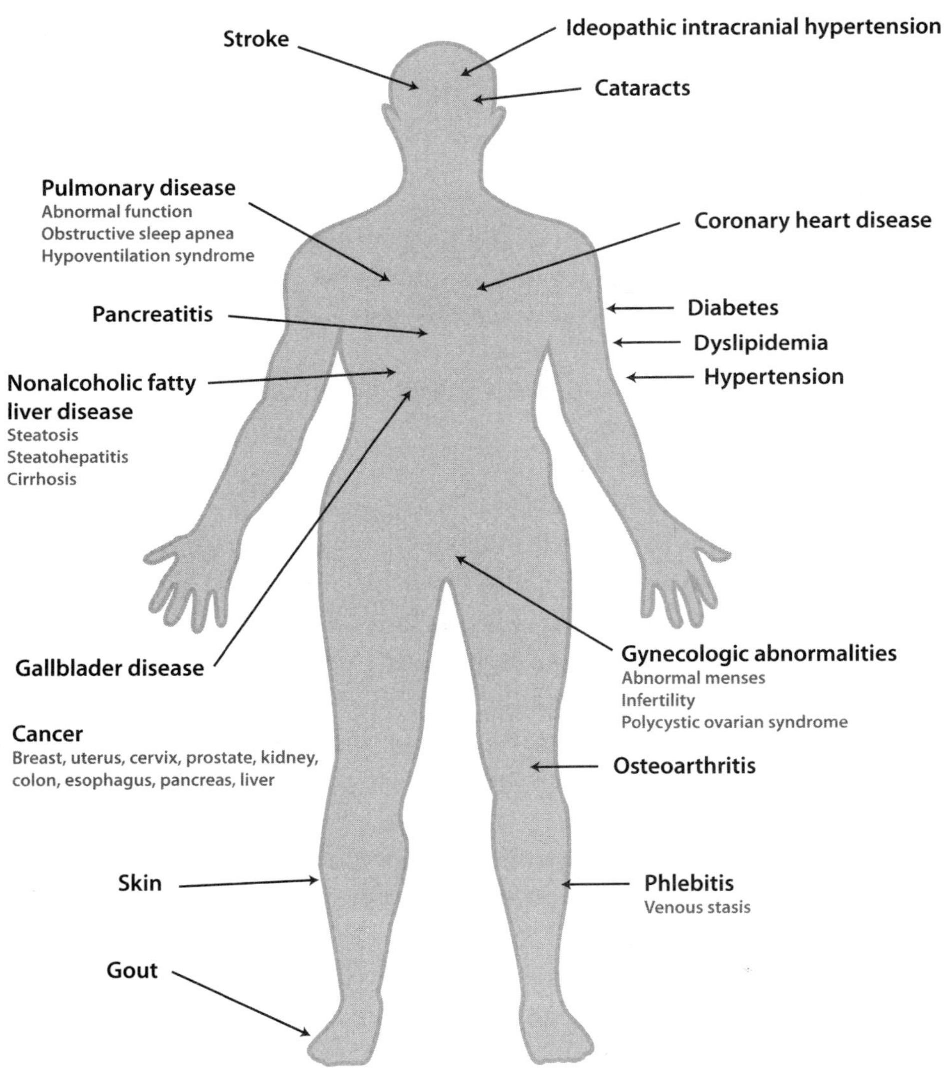

WHEN WE CONTINUE TO FEED OUR BODY MORE ENERGY THAN IT NEEDS . . .

Fat cells are driven to reproduce themselves

Tension and infighting between the fat cells and pancreas occurs

The body begins storing fat in the blood vessel walls, leading to plaque formation

Our heart, blood vessels, and joints are put under increased stress

THE DAY OF **MY AWAKENING**

One morning several years ago, I had my own wake-up call. While stepping out of the shower, I unexpectedly caught a glimpse of my reflection in the mirror. Just days before, I had calculated my BMI and found it to be 34.4—a number squarely in the obese category. Initially I thought, *The research scientists who developed this index table must have miscalculated their numbers. I'm not fat.* Then I hesitantly looked at a table that revealed the inevitable consequences and medical conditions that accompany obesity, and I was not a happy camper.

So there I was, standing naked and looking at my reflection in the mirror. I almost jumped out of my skin! There was a middle-aged, "jiggly," bloated man looking back at me! I said to my wife, "Wow! I have really gotten fat!" I was crushed, but in that moment I realized the BMI index must be true—I was obese. But how could this be? How had I let myself get that far out of control?

That day, I stepped out of the dugout of life and into the Game of Health. My first step was becoming keenly *aware* of my condition. I set out on my first trip around the bases, although I didn't realize that was what I was doing at the time. I had to discover what changes I needed to make. Soon I began to understand there were several reasons for my fitness demise. The biggest problem I found was that I was eating too much food. Not only did I have a *quantity* issue, I also had a *quality* issue. I desperately needed to make some changes.

THE POWER OF **CHANGING HABITS**

Losing weight is not as simple as calories in, calories out—although it is one key. What you eat, how much you eat, your activity level, the relationships in your life, the amount of sleep and water you get and your sense of purpose all play significant roles. For me, I had significant issues.

To change the condition of my body, I needed to change many of my eating habits. One of the first habits I had to eliminate from my daily routine was my 10 a.m. trip to the Cookie Bouquet. Every day I started with my first patient at 7 a.m. By 10 a.m. I was usually very hungry. The Pop Tart, candy bar, bagel, popular cereal, or white toast with jam I was eating for breakfast was not providing the nourishment I needed. These foods actually made my hunger worse because they are refined, simple carbohydrates. They flood the bloodstream with sugar and then leave a person feeling famished within a couple of hours.

That was the condition I was in around 10 a.m. Consequently, I would shoot out the back door of my office and race down to the Cookie Bouquet for a Diet Coke and a cookie. The cookie itself was probably 500 calories, which meant I would need to take about 7,000 steps to burn it off. Unfortunately, I averaged a mere 4,500 steps a day at that time—not even enough to work off the cookie. Cutting refined, high sugar calories like this out of my diet explains at least 10 of the 50 pounds that I eventually lost.

A HEALTHY SNACK

Fresh fruit is a great snack. If you can't get fresh fruit, get dried fruit. They usually come in handy, resealable packages. Dried fruit also has a long shelf life and doesn't need to be refrigerated.

In addition to *eating fewer calories*, the other key to losing weight is moving more—increasing our Training. Habits that helped me put these two principles into practice were formed one choice at a time. Finding motivation to eat healthier became easier for me once I started to pay close attention to the calorie content and portion sizes of my food. For me, this began by refocusing my attention on reading food labels.

READ THE LABEL

Cola Nutrition Facts

Serving Size: 12 fl oz
Serving Per Container

Amount Per Serving		
Calories 150		Calories from Fat 0
		% Daily Value
Total Fat 0 g		0%
Saturated Fat	0 g	0%
Trans Fat	0 g	
Cholesterol		
Sodium 35 mg		
Potassium 46.5 mg		
Total Carbohydrate 0.15 g		
Dietary Fiber		
Sugars		
Sugar Alcohols		
Protein 0 g		
Vitamin A		
Vitamin C		
Calcium		
Iron		

Establishing a habit of reading the nutrition label on foods is a powerful step toward a healthier you. Yes, it may seem a bit intimidating at first, but with a little practice you can learn to accurately determine the amount of calories you are eating and the value they contain. For example, look at the sample food label for a common can of cola. At the top of the label you will see how the manufacturer estimates a portion. In this case, a 12-ounce can of cola is *one serving*. Often, there are two or more servings in one package. For instance, sometimes half of a candy bar is considered one portion. In a situation like that, you would need to double the nutritional information provided on the label if you ate the whole candy bar.

Food labels also reveal the total number of calories per serving. There are 150 calories in this can of cola. For an average person to burn this amount of calories, he would need to walk about 1 mile or take 2,000 steps. If you take in additional calories from snacks like this soda and do not accommodate for them by increasing your amount of training, every 23 days you will take in an additional 3,500 calories. That equals one pound of additional weight. If you did this for one year, you would gain about 15 pounds!

This simple calculation can be performed with any food. They all follow the same rules. Realize that eating calorie-rich foods increases the chance that our fat cells will become overloaded. We will learn more about calories in the sections ahead, but for now establish a habit of reading the food label. Whenever you eat, think about the caloric information and make an effort to choose better foods.

SLOW DOWN AND LET YOUR STOMACH STRETCH

So I began eating fewer calories, increasing my physical activity, and reading food labels. Another thing I did to improve the shape I was in was reduce the quantity of food I was eating. You too may have a problem with the quantity of food you are eating. One of the reasons we eat too much is because *we eat too fast*. By simply slowing down while we eat, we will eat less. Why? Because we will begin to feel full.

Realize that when we eat, our stomach stretches to make room for the food. This stretching stimulates a series of nerves running from the stomach to the brain, telling the brain we are full. Normally, our empty stomach is the size of our fist, so you can see that filling and stretching it is not a difficult task. Drinking a glass of water, skim milk or tea between meals is a healthy way to stretch your stomach and feel full.

You feel full in response to your stomach stretching. Some healthy ways to stretch your stomach and make it feel full include drinking a cup of water, tea, or skim milk or eating raw vegetables between meals.

Another major reason we begin to feel full is linked to the fat we eat. Fat stimulates the release of hormones from our gut, which travel through the bloodstream to the brain and tell us we are full. We will discuss fats in more detail in the next section on Oil.

Additionally, if a person has had the lap band surgery and has a band around the top portion of their stomach, it will help curb their appetite. This means the upper part of their stomach will stretch with a much smaller meal, causing them to feel full. When we feel full, we eat less, and when we eat less, we lose weight. This is the reason for the success of this surgery many are having today. Interestingly, if we chronically overeat, the amount of stretching required to feel full will increase over time.

Try to avoid getting second helpings. You have fed your body. Give it time to figure out that it has enough energy on board. Allow your body's hormones stimulated by your food to tell your brain you are full. If you are still hungry after 15 minutes, eat another helping of vegetables. For every helping of anything else—bread, pasta, potatoes, rice, meat—you will need to add 500 or more steps to your daily goal.

Armed with all this information, I began doing things to help myself resist the temptation to overeat. First, I started serving myself in the kitchen and did not bring the serving dishes with the starchy or fattening foods to the table. That way the calorie- or starch-rich food was not sitting right in front of me calling my name. If I wanted more, I would have to get up and walk to the kitchen. This gave me time to consciously pay attention to my body and decide if I really wanted a second helping. Trust me, it works. You can do it too.

LEARN TO USE **THE HAND SIGNALS OF HEALTH**

The other habit I cultivated was to use my hands to measure the serving sizes of what I was eating. Thus, the *Hand Signals of Health* were created. Food is divided into four general categories: meat, carbohydrates, vegetables and dessert. As a rule, the amount of meat we eat should be the size of the palm of our hand and as thick as a deck of cards. Vegetables—except for starchy ones like potatoes and corn—are free food. We can fill our plate with as much as we want. As for carbohydrates like bread, pasta, potatoes, corn and rice, the serving size should be no larger than the width of our fingers and about as tall as your fist.

When we finish with our first plate, we need to stop and take a time out—about 15 to 20 minutes. This allows our stretching stomach to send our brain the signal that we are full. After this allotment of time, IF we are still HUNGRY, we can then have a second portion. But seconds come with a price. Vegetables are still free, but everything else must be compensated for with additional activity or exercise. For example, a second helping of bread or meat constitutes a half mile walk per portion (750-1,000 steps).

Palm of Hand	**appropriate portion of lean/low-fat MEAT. Try to make it no thicker than a deck of cards.**
Width of Fingers	**appropriate portion of CARBOHYDRATES, such as bread, pasta, potatoes, corn and rice. It should be about as tall as your fist.**
Vegetables	**except for starchy ones like potatoes and corn, these are free food. Fill your plate, but avoid high-fat sauces, butter, oils, etc.**

If we decide to forgo seconds but choose to have dessert, then one *sliver* of pie or cake (no thicker than the width of one finger) equals one mile (about 2,000 steps). If we eat a *slice* (the width of two fingers), we must double that mileage, and for a *piece* of dessert (three fingers), triple it and so on.

The bottom line: Extra calories should equal extra Training or exercise. If it doesn't, extra calories will equal extra weight. When Roundness goes up, problems result. You may think this all sounds very harsh, but it is all a matter of balancing food with activity. For me, if I have had an active day and/or gone to the gym and exercised and I want a sliver, slice or piece of dessert, then I have it! Healthy living is about balance, not deprivation.

DESSERT ANYONE?

A **SLIVER**	**of pie or cake, no thicker than the width of your finger = about 1 mile or 2,000 steps**
A **SLICE**	**of dessert, about the width of two fingers = 2 miles or 4,000 steps.**
A **PIECE**	**of dessert, about the width of three fingers = 3 miles or 6,000 steps**

Extra calories should equal extra Training or exercise. If not, they equal extra weight.

REALIZE **T AND R DIRECTLY AFFECT OU AND B**

At this point you can see how a lack of Training and the gradual accumulation of a round girth set the stage for a TROUBLING future. When the amount of energy we take in continues to exceed our body's need and our fat cells are full, we create a raging metabolic war inside our body. If you fail to take heed and continue to allow your Roundness to increase and your Training to decrease, your system will begin to show signs of wear and tear. This may come in the form of high blood pressure first, followed by a cholesterol abnormality or diabetes.[4]

The third, fourth and fifth numbers that will save your life are *Oil, Unacceptable Sugar,* and *Blood Pressure*. Your daily amount of Training or activity not only affects your Roundness, it also profoundly affects these three areas. As you work through the next three sections, you will learn which numbers reveal certain things about your body.

The first step to keeping your Roundness in check is to **use a pedometer daily**. It will help you monitor and increase your quantity of Training. Remember, *all activity counts*! The break-even point is 6,000 steps, and 10,000 steps is the goal to aim for if you are trying to lose weight. If you are below these numbers, don't get upset with yourself. Make a decision to gradually increase your number of steps daily until you reach the desired goal.

I also encourage you to **weigh yourself regularly**. I do this daily, but many experts believe that weekly works better for most people. I don't lose sleep if my weight is not where I want it to be. The number on the scale is a *lagging*, not leading, indicator of good health. By checking your weight regularly, you can monitor and correct your course to ensure what you're doing is successful.

---

4 Many individuals get high cholesterol, diabetes or hypertension without being overweight or obese. For example type 1 diabetes appears to be an interaction of a person's genetic make-up with their environment, like a viral infection. What I hope to help people prevent is what occurs in a human being when their genetic makeup interacts with the environment in the form of excess caloric intake. This differentiation is more than cosmetic. We treat these conditions differently and they follow a different natural history than the path that I am writing about in this book. I would strongly encourage anyone with any of these conditions to seek medical help regarding your condition.

Another way a person can look at their weight is by looking at their waist circumference. This is particularly important because the fat in your abdomen is actually more destructive than the fat under the skin. So on average if a woman has a waist circumference of over 35 inches she has a significant amount of this abdominal fat - significantly increasing her risk of problems. Between 30 and 35 inches suggests intermediate risk. Less than 30 is usually not associated with significantly increased risk (by checking the actual OUB numbers we will see if this is the case for you). For men the numbers are > 40 inches, 36 - 40 inches and < 36 inches. These rough estimates can be a helpful guide. For instruction on how to measure your waist circumference go to **www.thesevennumbers.com**.

And by all means, **incorporate the Hand Signals of Health** at each meal and remember to **read those food labels**. These two activities will help you control the quantity and quality of calories you are taking into your body. Interestingly, most of us only eat ten to twenty different foods over and over again in different combinations. Take a few minutes and write a list of your main menu choices. Then over the next week, look up the nutritional information on them. Take note of how many calories they have as well as the amount of protein, sugar, fat, fiber, etc. As we learn about the remaining numbers, you will discover areas where opportunities for improvement exist. Every healthy food choice you make is a step in the right direction.

STEPS IN THE RIGHT DIRECTION

Use a pedometer daily.

Weigh yourself regularly.

Incorporate the Hand Signals of Health at each meal.

Read those food labels.

ROUNDNESS: PRESSING TOWARD THE GOAL

	POOR	IMPROVING	ACHIEVING EXCELLENCE
Body Mass Index (BMI)	Greater than 30	25 to 29	Less than 25
Percentage of Body Fat	Men > 25% Women > 32%	Men 19-25% Women 26-32%	Men < 19% Women < 26%
Waist Circumference	Men > 40in Women > 35in	Men 36-40 in Women 30-35 in	Men < 36 in Women < 30 in

PLAYING THE GAME OF HEALTH

5 STEPS TO MAKING ROUNDNESS YOUR OWN

AWARENESS: What is your BMI? Is it poor, improving, or achieving excellence? Do you know how many calories you are taking in on a given day? Are you taking in more than you are burning? What practical things can you do to lower your BMI and the number of calories you are taking in?

UNDERSTANDING: Can you see how a lack of Training increases Roundness and causes major health problems? Which problems caught your attention most? Are you currently experiencing any of these? What benefits of Training would you like to experience more of in your life?

HABITS: What unhealthy habits do you have that are keeping you from Training and/or causing you to over-eat? How can you eliminate these and start taking more responsibility for your health? What can you do to incorporate the Hand Signals of Health and begin reading food labels?

ACCOUNTABILITY: Who can you ask to hold you accountable regarding your Training and eating? If you have a spouse or child living with you, consider asking them for help as well, since they will most likely be with you at mealtime.

SHARING: In your Training journal, record your meals and portion sizes, as well as your activities. Do this for only one month so you can see your progress. Once you begin to see some positive progress, look for others with whom you can share what you are learning.

NUMBER THREE

"Yes, there is such a thing as *good* fat. Your body needs fat! The good types of fat heal the body and are necessary. You should eat fat every day for the health of your heart, brain, skin, hair, and every part of you. Good fat nourishes and strengthens cell membranes. Good fats include Monounsaturated fats and Omega-3 fats. …The fats you should avoid are trans fatty acids, often called 'trans fats,' such as hydrogenated and partially hydrogenated fats. You need to limit your consumption of saturated and polyunsaturated fats."

Don Colbert, M.D.

Don Colbert, M.D., *The Seven Pillars of Health* (Lake Mary, FL: Siloam, a Strang Publication, 2007) pp. 96, 87.

OIL

The **O** in our TROUBLE Assessment stands for *Oil.* It is the quantity and quality of *fats* we have in our body. While too much of the wrong fat can be deadly, not having enough of the right fat can also pose problems. Oil plays a vital role in the human body. It surrounds every cell like an envelope, separating the inside from the outside. Oil is also the building block of our hormones—the internal messengers that tell our body how to function. Oil surrounds our nerve cells, allowing rapid communication from our head to our toes. Needless to say, trying to live life on a very low-fat (low-oil) diet is not sensible and could throw our whole system out of balance. We need healthy fat in our diet every day.

UNDERSTANDING THE **THREE MAIN TYPES OF FAT**

Saturated Fat: tends to increase the LDL (lethal) cholesterol. Hydrogenated and partially hydrogenated foods contain trans fatty acids and polyunsaturated fat that have a similar effect to saturated fat.

Polyunsaturated Fat: not as likely to cause problems, but not the healthiest form of fat.

Monounsaturated Fat: The healthiest type of fat.

Avoid saturated fat as much as possible. Limit eating polyunsaturated fat. Consume monounsaturated fat on a regular basis.

It is important to understand that fat in our food comes packaged in three main forms: Saturated fat, polyunsaturated fat and monounsaturated fat. Let's take a closer look at each.

SATURATED FAT: In general, this fat is not good because it increases the level of LDL, or lethal fat, in the body. Saturated fat becomes solid at room temperature. It is the densest source of energy we can consume. Once broken down in the body, it tends to increase the amount of LDL cholesterol in our system. LDL is the lethal cholesterol that is bad for our body. Butter, coconut oil, palm kernel oil, palm oil, and animal fat (lard) are examples of saturated fats.

POLYUNSATURATED FAT: These are the intermediate density fats that, in general, are not as likely to cause problems in the body. Polyunsaturated fats tend to be liquid at room temperature. Examples of these are corn oil, cottonseed oil, flaxseed oil, rapeseed oil, safflower oil, sesame oil, soybean oil, sunflower oil and fish oil, which also contain the beneficial nutrients DHA and EPA.

MONOUNSATURATED FAT: Of the three main fats, these are the healthiest and best choice. The most common sources are avocados, peanuts, almonds, macadamias, canola oil, and olive oil and products containing olive oil. The Mediterranean diet is high in monounsaturated fat and has attracted a lot of positive attention in the medical community over the past several years. It includes olive oil and many olive products. The Lyon Heart Study showed that patients who had a high risk of heart disease and ate the Mediterranean diet as opposed to a regular low-fat diet experienced a 70 percent reduction in the occurrence of heart attacks. The exact reason for this remains a mystery, but the healthy effects this type of diet has on blood clots and blood vessels may be partially responsible.

What about hydrogenated and partially hydrogenated oil? Good question. Hydrogenated and partially hydrogenated oil is man-made. Food engineers have discovered that by adding extra molecules of hydrogen to certain oils, it keeps them from becoming rancid. This means prepared foods last longer before spoiling, and a longer shelf life means higher profits. Unfortunately, hydrogenated fats are unstable and change into trans fatty acids once in the body. The body then handles these substances like saturated fat, making them less beneficial. It is safe to assume that if the food comes in a sealed box or bag, it is more likely to contain hydrogenated fat. These will be listed in the ingredients on any food label.

The bottom line: When it comes to fat, avoid saturated fat as much as possible and consume monounsaturated fat regularly in moderation. Polyunsaturated fats are fine with a few exceptions. If they are heated, they produce dangerous particles called free radicals that can damage our body's tissues. This occurs when foods are fried in polyunsaturated oils. So for frying foods, use olive, peanut, or canola oil.

WORST	**SATURATED FATS** **Animal fat, butter, coconut oil, palm oil**
BETTER	**POLYUNSATURATED FATS** **Corn oil, cottonseed oil, flaxseed oil, rapeseed oil, sesame oil, soybean oil, sunflower oil**
BEST	**MONOUNSATURATED FATS** **Olive oil, peanut oil, canola oil**

HOW **OUR BODY BREAKS DOWN AND USES FAT**

The nutrients from food must be transported to the cells of the body. As I mentioned earlier, when food is eaten, it is broken down in the mouth, stomach and then small intestine. In the case of fats, they are broken down into *glycerol* and, to a lesser degree, *cholesterol*. These smaller droplets of fat then float up the portal vein in the bloodstream on a carrier molecule called a chilomicron. Eventually the fat, which is energy, is dropped off with cells in the body that need energy. If cells do not need energy, the fat is carried to the liver where it is repackaged and placed on another carrier, or "vehicle," called VLDL (very low density lipoproteins).

Don't be intimidated by the terms chilomicron and VLDL. They are nothing more than microscopic "trucks" that carry fat to the cells of the body that need it. Once they deliver their load to our tissues, particularly muscles and fat cells, these carriers become smaller and smaller. After a while, they become so small and so different in their composition that they are renamed remnant particles or *LDL* (low density lipoproteins). Ideally, these remnants are taken to the liver and repackaged into new VLDL.

UNDERSTANDING **HOW PLAQUE FORMS**

The formation of LDL is where the potential for problems begins. Although the most desirable destination is back to the liver, LDL can go a number of other places in the body. If there is more LDL floating around the blood than the liver can take in, which often occurs when you overeat or your fat cells are full, then the LDL molecules may pass through the wall of the blood vessel and attach itself there. This is the process known as *plaque formation* (also known as atherogenesis and atherosclerosis). Simply put, this is the buildup of fat in the blood vessel wall.

For now it is enough to say that this process will gum up our blood vessels and cause problems (check out the section on Exploding Plaque or go to **www.thesevennumbers.com** and watch the Follow the Food video). The rate at which this buildup takes place is directly proportional to the amount of extra energy (fat) left in the blood after the cells in our body absorb what they can. As I mentioned earlier, if Training decreases and food consumption remains the same or increases, the buildup of plaque in the arteries will accelerate. This is especially true if we are eating high-fat, calorie-rich foods. There is simply no place for the extra energy (fat) to go. The results are extra LDL floating around in the blood. This is a lethal situation that must be dealt with quickly, and increased Training is just what the doctor ordered.

THE AWESOME **EFFECTS OF TRAINING**

As I mentioned in the chapter on Training, one of the greatest effects of exercise is that it "cleans" our blood. When we exercise, our muscles become hungry for energy. Two sources can provide us with the needed energy. The quickest form of energy is glucose. It can be pulled out of the blood, drawn from that which is stored in the muscle itself, or extracted from the liver when it is made or from glycogen that is broken down.

Once sugar is used up, the muscle cells begin to use fat for energy. The muscles pull the fat off of the chilomicrons and VLDL carrier molecules floating in the blood and use it for energy to keep you moving. Training activates this blood-cleaning process, which continues for twenty-four to forty-eight hours *after* you exercise. The removal of excess energy from the blood helps prevent the accumulation of lethal LDL in the artery walls.

Exercise causes the body to redistribute its energy, and a key player in this process is another "carrier" molecule called HDL. This special transporter races through our body and scrapes up all the fat it can find to be used as energy. It even goes into the blood vessel walls and harvests fat! This explains why HDL is so valuable and we do everything we can to get this healthy cholesterol carrier to increase in our body. Do you know what drives up HDL levels most? You got it—exercise. Indeed, it is ***the best medicine for your body!***

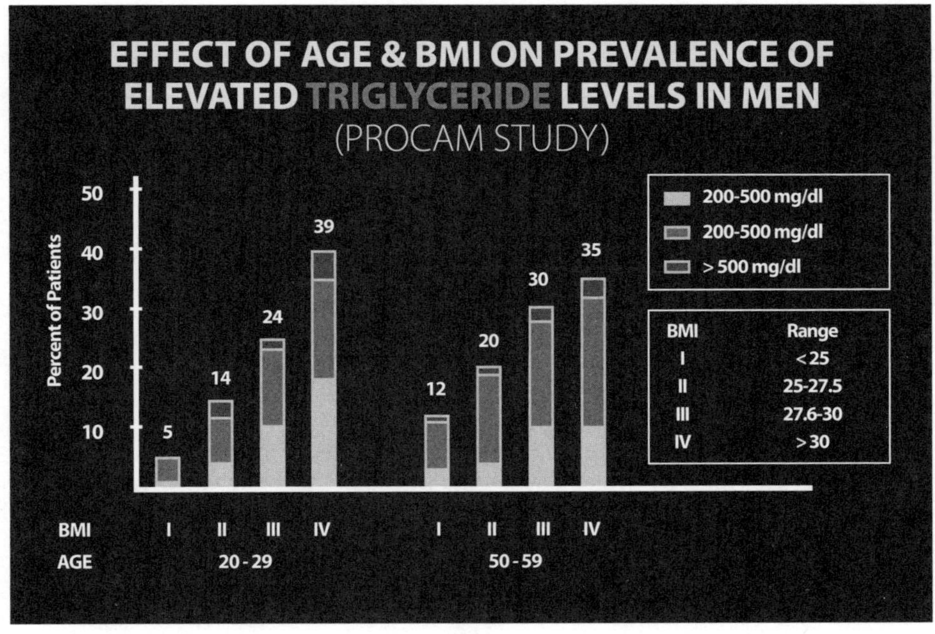

Adapted from Assmann and Schulte. In: Bjorntorp P and Brodoff B, eds. Obesity, 1992

This chart shows how fat (triglycerides) builds up in the bloodstream as we get heavier. Whether you are in your 20s or your 50s, as you become overweight and obese, the body has more difficulty "cleaning" the blood and removing the extra fats. These extra fats have a significant effect and can lead to plaque formation in our arteries.

DISCOVERING **THE ROLE OF CALORIES**

At this point, you may be thinking, *Where do calories fit into this equation? How are they connected with oil, energy and Training?* Calories are a measurement of the amount of energy in a given food. Different foods have different amounts of energy, or calories. The average man needs about 1,800 - 2,500 calories a day and the average woman needs about 1,300 - 2,000 calories a day to function properly. This can be calculated many ways. Please go to **www.thesevennumbers.com** for more information.

When the amount of activity we perform in a given day is *less* than the amount of calories we take in, we *gain* weight. When the amount of activity *exceeds* the amount of calories we take in, we *lose* weight. This is why regular Training is so vital to weight loss.

Each activity we are involved in burns a certain number of calories. For instance, the brain uses approximately 20 percent of the total number of calories we consume daily to carry out its functions. The energy it consumes is primarily in the form of glucose (sugar) because it cannot use fat as a direct energy source under normal circumstances. One would think that we could increase the consumption of sugar from our body by thinking harder or longer, but that is not the case. Evidently, the amount of energy needed to stay awake and concentrate doesn't change enough to make a significant impact on our energy consumption. Too bad!

How about walking? At a leisurely pace, this activity "burns" about 100 calories in one mile. In other words, our muscles need roughly 100 calories of energy to propel our body one mile. Said another way, our muscles will extract 100 calories of sugar or fat for every mile that we walk. Thirty minutes of dancing will burn about 140 calories, and thirty minutes of gardening will consume about 165. (For more activity values, go to **www.thesevennumbers.com**.)

So how much broccoli would we need to eat to leisurely walk a mile? The answer is about two cups because broccoli contains about 27 calories per half cup. On the other hand, a regular Snickers bar contains 240 calories. This one bar is enough to propel us 2.4 miles. How about cheesecake? One piece contains 400 to 800 calories, depending on the type. My favorite cheesecake used to be from The Cheesecake Factory until I learned it contained 880 calories! That means eating one piece of cheesecake would require walking 8 miles to burn it off. As you can see, some food packs quite a punch! We really need to count the cost before putting something in our mouths.

To increase the amount of calories we burn while walking, we can simply walk faster, further, or on more difficult terrain, such as hills or mountains. We can also burn more calories by carrying weights. This puts other muscles to work, increasing the demand for energy. Any time you use your muscles, you clear energy in the form of fat and sugar from your bloodstream. Clearly, Training produces some awesome effects and really helps trim the fat from our body.

Each activity we are involved in burns a certain number of calories. When the amount of activity we perform in a given day is less than the amount of calories we take in, we gain weight. When the amount of activity exceeds the amount of calories we take in, we lose weight.

FIND OUT **YOUR FAT NUMBERS**

Okay, so how can we find out the oil levels in our body? What do we need to do to determine how much LDL, HDL and triglycerides are floating around in our system? The answer is, go and get a *lipid panel test* done. Lipid is simply another name for fat. Your fat numbers can be determined through a simple blood test at your doctor's office, a health fair, or the blood bank where you give blood. Not only will they provide you with your LDL, HDL and triglyceride numbers, but they will also give you your total cholesterol count.

To help you understand your numbers, let's connect each one with the job it performs. I like to think of LDL as the lethal, low-down or lousy form of cholesterol. It's the potential *bad* guys, and its job is to carry fat *to* the cells for storage via the bloodstream. HDL, on the other hand, is the heavenly, happy or healthy cholesterol. It's the *good* guy that is activated by Training (exercise). Its job is to search out and scrape up fat from our body's cells and the walls of our arteries and bring it to the muscles to burn as energy. Triglycerides and free fatty acids are the names given to the particles of fat that float around in the blood to be used at any moment.

UNDERSTAND YOUR FAT NUMBERS

HDL is the heavenly, healthy, happy, good cholesterol

LDL is the lousy, lethal, low-down bad cholesterol

Triglycerides are free floating molecules of fat energy that can be directly used by our cells

When you exercise, your muscles pull energy in the form of sugar and fat from your blood

If we were to go to a highly active, agrarian (farming) society, we would find a clear connection between physical labor, healthy foods and healthy blood. Their diets would probably consist of highly complex carbohydrates, such as beans, whole grains, vegetables, and/or fruit. Their protein sources would be lean meats, like fowl, fish, wild rabbit, deer, squirrel, or free range cattle. As a result of their diet and highly active lifestyle, their HDL/LDL/triglycerides numbers would probably come back around 70/70/70. With fat numbers like these, people rarely, if ever, die of heart disease or stroke.

On the contrary, if we were to go a sedentary or low-activity society, such as the United States, we would find a clear connection between low physical activity, unhealthy foods and unhealthy blood. Here at home, our diet consists of less complex carbohydrates. Foods are more refined and processed and contain an increased amount of saturated and trans fats. Our sources of protein are fattier meats such as highly marbled beef and pork.

As a result, our HDL levels are low, and our LDL and triglycerides levels are high.

As HDL levels drop below 60 in women and below 50 in men, we know that blood vessels are less protected and more at risk to develop plaque formation. When HDL levels drop below 50 in women and below 40 in men, we know that the HDL no longer has a protective value in the body. As HDL levels drop, LDL levels rise. As LDL levels move up from 70, the likelihood that fat will get stuck in blood vessel walls increases. Keeping our HDL level high is vital. Studies like the one done on the Framingham Men (shown on the next page) reveal that even in the presence of high amounts of LDL, if HDL levels are high, the risk of death from heart attack or stroke is drastically lower.

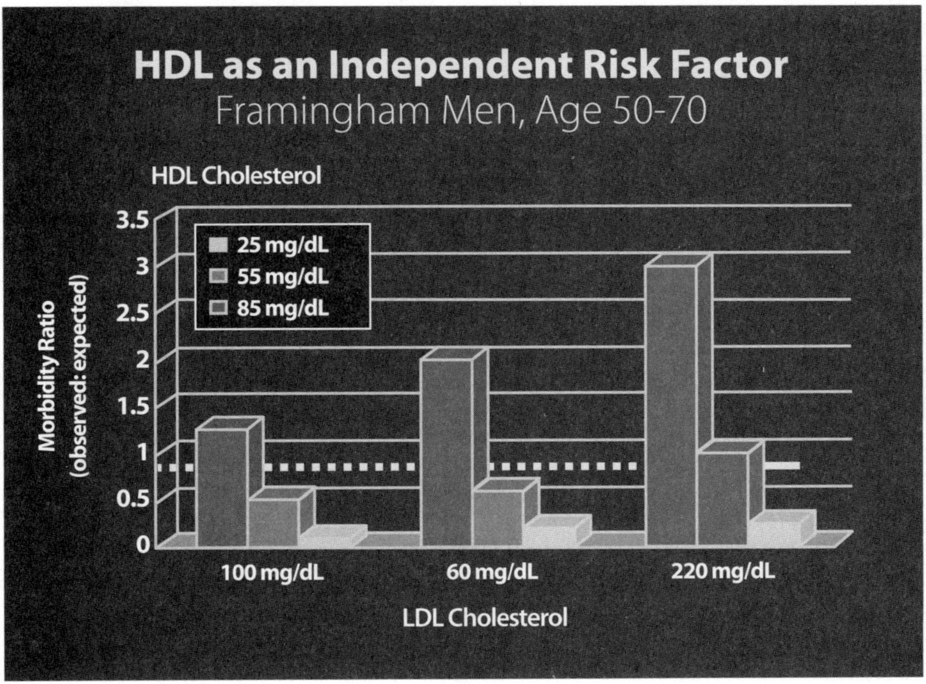

The medical industry has established two cutoff points at which they recommend medication. If a person has *never had* a heart attack or stroke, we prescribe cholesterol controlling medicine for an LDL level of 130. If a person *has had* a heart attack or stroke, we prescribe cholesterol controlling medicine for an LDL level over 100. Triglycerides are a little harder to figure out as their correlation with heart disease is not as clear. These fats are more variable and affected by many other factors, so we are less focused on them. However, if they rise over 150, they are considered too high, and treatment with a vitamin (niacin) or medication may be warranted.

The ideal fat numbers are: LDL less than 70; HDL greater than 60 in women and greater than 50 in men; and a triglycerides level of less than 90. To get the Total Cholesterol count, we take the HDL + LDL + [triglycerides / 5]. Historically, a Total Cholesterol count below 200 has been considered healthy. However, because this number alone can sometimes be misleading, we use a ratio of the Total Cholesterol / HDL to get an accurate reading of our fat levels. This lets us know how many good guys (HDL) we have in relation to the bad guys (LDL). The Ideal ratio we aim for is less than 3.0. Any ratio greater than 5 is a major concern that may require intervention.

The ideal fat numbers are: LDL less than 70; HDL greater than 60 in women and greater than 50 in men; and a triglyceride level of less than 90.

MAKE SURE YOU **READ THOSE LABELS**

Next to increasing your Training, watching what you eat is a major key to maintaining healthy oil levels. I've said it before and I'll say it again: Make sure you *read the labels*. I know they may seem a bit intimidating at first, but they are really not hard to understand. Take a look at the food label for a pre-prepared steak and biscuit meal. For now, let's focus our attention on the fat and calorie content.

Steak with biscuit
Nutrition Facts

Serving Size: 1 serving	
Serving Per Container	
Amount Per Serving	
Calories 455	Calories from Fat 234
	% Daily Value
Total Fat 26 g	0%
Saturated Fat 6.9 g	0%
Monosaturated fat 11.1 g	
Polynsaturated Fat 6.4 g	
Cholesterol 25 mg	
Sodium 795 mg	
Total Carbohydrate 44.4 g	
Dietary Fiber 0 g	
Sugars 0 g	
Protein 13.1 g	

As you look at the label, notice the total calories— 455. This is nearly one-third of the total daily recommended number of calories for a woman. Under the fat section, we see the three types of fat broken down. In this instance, the *saturated fat* is 6.9 grams, the *polyunsaturated* fat is 6.4 grams, and the *monounsaturated* fat is 11.1 grams. As a general rule, you want to keep the saturated fat as close to zero as possible (< 7 percent for daily calories is the American Heart Association guideline). If it is a fried food or contains hydrogenated or partially hydrogenated oil, you want to keep the polyunsaturated as close to zero as well. I do want to give you a major warning: Fat in any form has the most calories per gram. There are 9 calories per gram of fat as compared to 4 to 5 calories per gram of carbohydrates and proteins.

This means for one gram of fat, you have to walk twice as many steps as you would to burn one gram of protein or carbohydrates. This is the reason why the popular diets during the 1980s and 1990s attempted to lower the calories by lowering the fat. The only problem with this is that fat provides the body with one of the strongest cues that it is full. This explains why someone on a low-fat diet will often experience a lot of hunger throughout the day. I have experienced this myself.

To get around this, I often eat a fat-containing snack around 4 p.m. Included in the snack is a handful of almonds—a good source of healthy monounsaturated fat. I found that eating the snack without almonds left me unbearably hungry in a short amount of time. Adding almonds helped me feel full longer. This allowed me to come home at night with my appetite under control instead of like a ravenous bear prone to overeating.

HEALTHY SNACK ITEMS

Almonds, pumpkin seeds, macadamia nuts, soy nuts
Plain yogurt (I like Greek yogurt.)
Applesauce with cinnamon, bananas with cinnamon and agave nectar
Apples, pears, grapes, strawberries, blueberries

As a general rule, you want to get 20 to 30 percent of your total calories each day from fat. If you are on a 1,500-calorie diet, this is about 300 to 450 calories or 33 to 50 total grams of fat each day. Eating a 26-gram steak and biscuit meal will wipe out most of the day's allotment. Remember, it is easier to avoid TROUBLE than to fix it after the fact. So read those labels. They will help you *buy* better foods and therefore *eat* better foods.

So there you have it. That is an overview of Oil in a nutshell. I encourage you to read over this chapter a couple of times to familiarize yourself with the information, and form a new habit of reading food labels. With the right knowledge and help from God above, you can discipline yourself to take in the good fats and steer clear of the bad ones.

OIL: PRESSING TOWARD THE GOAL

TYPE OF FAT	POOR	IMPROVING	ACHIEVING EXCELLENCE
LDL [Lethal, Bad]	Greater than 130	70 to 100	Less than 70
HDL [Heav-enly, Good]	Women: Less than 50 | Men: Less than 40	Women: 50 to 60 | Men: 40 to 50	Women: Greater than 60 | Men: Greater than 50
Triglycerides	Greater than 150	90 to 150	Less than 90
HDL/Total Cholesterol Ratio	Greater than 5	3.5 to 5	Less than 3.5

PLAYING THE GAME OF HEALTH

5 STEPS TO ENSURE YOU ARE GETTING THE RIGHT QUANTITY AND QUALITY OF OIL

AWARENESS: Are you eating foods with unhealthy, saturated fats? Are you eating any foods with good, monounsaturated fats? Look in your cupboard and take note of the different types of cooking oils you have. What is your HDL (good fat) level and your LDL (bad fat) level? If you don't know, a trip to your doctor for some blood work is definitely in order.

UNDERSTANDING: Do you have a clear picture of the problems associated with consuming saturated fats? Can you see how eliminating saturated fat and increasing your consumption of healthy, monounsaturated fat can improve your quality of life? What are some ways that you can eliminate some of the more dangerous oils in your diet?

HABITS: One of the best habits to develop is planning a weekly menu. Go to a local bookstore or supermarket and look through some "cooking light" cookbooks. Get ideas of better, healthier ways to prepare your meals. Plan breakfast, lunch and dinner for the week, using healthy, monounsaturated fats whenever possible. Make a quick list of fast food restaurants that offer the healthiest foods.

ACCOUNTABILITY: Ladies, get together with some of your friends and put together a list of recipes that use less unhealthy oil and more healthy oil. Start experimenting together. Husbands, ask your wife if she will help you lose weight by finding some recipes that are lower in fat. If you are overweight and out of shape, she will probably be relieved to hear you are taking this kind of interest in your health. [Note: Knowing that many men enjoy doing the cooking, these instructions work both ways.]

SHARING: Once you become more aware of the importance of good oils and understand the dangers associated with unhealthy fats, begin to share with friends and family some of the insights you have learned. If you are bringing a dish to a family reunion or a get-together with friends, bring a healthier alternative, such as a veggie or fruit tray instead of a casserole or dessert.

Don't Die-it —Live It!

Without a good understanding of fats and why we need them, many Americans have fallen prey to myriads of quick-fix, fad diets that have not worked. Consequently, they have been left feeling frustrated, hopeless and sometimes ill. To help you avoid this as well as other harmful effects, here are a few things to consider about fad diets and eating habits.

Most diets oversimplify complex issues. Not all of us are heavy for the same reason. Some of us are overweight because we overeat relatively healthy food. Others eat too much fat. Some are on a sugar roller coaster or take medication that leads to weight gain. Others simply don't exercise, or feed their anxiety, stress, or depression with food. For many, it is a combination of two or more of these reasons. True change comes when we look at an overview of our behavior and make adjustments in several areas.

Most diets teach a gimmick. Oh, it may work, but it does not lead to a lifestyle change in the way you eat and exercise. Sure, we can eat only grapefruit for a week and lose 7 pounds. But more than likely, we will quickly end up in the same old eating pattern as before.

Most diets are impossible to maintain. They place restrictions on your eating that are impossible to continue for a long period of time. I mean, who can eat only sausage and eggs or oatmeal with skim milk for the rest of their lives? Eliminating carbohydrates, protein or fat will never work. We all need a variety of options to be successful.

Most diets add activities to already overcrowded schedules. This includes things like joining a gym, preparing special meals, exercising for extended periods or going to group meetings. We all live full, and sometimes hectic, lives. Just adding more activities is not the answer. We must take an honest look at what we're doing and make some adjustments to be successful.

Most diets eliminate fast food. Knowing the highly active American lifestyle, this will more than likely not work. Knowing what we are going to order *before* we pull up to the drive-thru window, reducing the number of times we eat out or learning to substitute better choices is more realistic and doable.

Most diets use a "one-size-fits-all" plan. But because each of us is a unique person, each body has its own set of rules. Add to this the changes in how our bodies operate through the different seasons of aging, and it is easy to see how one set diet regimen is not going to work for everyone. A post-menopausal woman is not going to respond to a diet the same way a twenty-five-year-old man will. Experimenting with different things until we find what works is the answer.

Most diets are built on unrealistic quick fixes. As I said earlier, there are no shortcuts to good health. It is through making a series of good choices over an extended period of time that results will come. Programs built on long-term, gradual, lifestyle changes will take weight off and keep it off.

For any diet to be successful, the suggested changes must be grounded in truth. If it sounds too good to be true, it probably is. Another major key to success is securing the support of your family and friends. Social support is vital; without it, no one will succeed. For more thoughts on this subject go to **www.mysevenhealers.com**.

NUMBER FOUR

"...Has anyone stopped to think about what happens to excess sugar that is the end product of carbohydrate metabolism? Some sugar is used in our blood to maintain an adequate circulating blood glucose level, and some will replenish glycogen stores in the liver and muscles. But what happens to the rest? It is converted to fat. Yes, most of our body fat comes from ingested sugar, not ingested fat. This conversion is facilitated by the hormone insulin."

H. Leighton Steward, Morrison C. Bethea, M.D., Samuel S. Andrews, M.D. and Luis A. Balart, M.D.

H. Leighton Steward, Morrison C. Bethea, M.D., Samuel S. Andrews, M.D. and Luis A. Balart, M.D., Sugar Busters! (New York, NY: The Ballantine Publishing Group, 1998) p. 102.

UNACCEPTABLE SUGAR

The **U** in our TROUBLE Assessment stands for *Unacceptable Sugar*. The numbers connected with Unacceptable Sugar show you how well your body is dealing with your intake of carbohydrates. Our body definitely needs sugar for energy to function properly. But too much sugar is a recipe for disaster we want to avoid.

One of the most interesting and controversial issues in medicine today is the effect refined carbohydrates, such as table sugar, has on our bodies. In his book *Sugar Blues*, William Duffy got this controversy going with his proclamation that the introduction of sugar has led to the collapse of every great society from Egypt to the present day. While many medical experts viewed this as fringe sensationalism, the publication of the book *Sugar Busters*! by H. Leighton Steward, Morrison Bethea, MD, Samuel Andrews, MD, and Luis Balart, MD, rekindled the flame.

Whether Duffy's claim is totally on target or not, the dramatic increase of refined sugar consumption and starchy foods by Americans is very concerning. According to the U.S. Department of Agriculture, the average American ate 5 pounds of sugar per year in 1900. In the year 2000, the estimated average sugar consumption per person was 163 pounds. That's a 3,260 percent increase in 100 years! Our sweet tooth is definitely out of control.

The numbers connected with Unacceptable Sugar show you how well your body is dealing with your intake of carbohydrates.

WHERE IS ALL THAT **SUGAR COMING FROM?**

How on earth could a person get all that sugar in their diet? Most of us may use a teaspoon here and there but never 163 pounds! Unfortunately, we are getting more sugar from our diet than we realize. As we have already discovered, processed foods are high in salt and sugar. If it is boxed up, wrapped in cellophane, and stored on a shelf for months at a time, it is highly processed and more than likely full of sugar, salt or fat. Sugar is often hidden under different names, such as corn syrup, high fructose corn syrup, maltose, dextrose, sucralose, and maltodextrin. If you read the labels, you will find it. These are nothing more than refined, and in some cases chemically engineered, sugars.

Prepared food items made from flour and sugar are another major source of sugar in our diet. This includes things like cookies, cakes, pies, candy, chips, ice cream, and soft drinks. Starchy foods are the other culprit. These come in the form of bread, pasta, corn, rice, and the biggest source, potatoes. In the past few years, there has been an increased emphasis on potatoes in our diet.

When we eat starchy foods like potatoes, pasta and corn, our body breaks them down into individual glucose molecules. These molecules quickly flow into the blood and raise our blood sugar level dramatically. Although this simple sugar is the main type our body uses for energy, too much sugar too fast puts a tremendous amount of stress on our body.

The average American ate 5 pounds of sugar in 1900. Today we eat about 163 pounds! In addition to refined sugars found in cookies, cakes, pies, candy, chips, ice cream, and soft drinks, the majority of our "sugars" come from bread, pasta, corn, rice and potatoes.

CARBS BREAK DOWN INTO **THREE MAIN FORMS OF SUGAR**

So, you might be thinking, *If sugar is a carbohydrate and carbohydrates have only half the calories of fat, why is eating carbs and sugar a problem?* The answer is not as simple as you might think. When we eat carbohydrates, they are broken down into three main forms of sugar: *glucose*, the most common; *fructose*, from table sugar, fruit and fruit juices; and *galactose*, from milk. Some carbohydrates, like fiber, cannot be broken down by our stomachs. Consequently, they form a significant portion of the bulk in our bowel movements. We will talk more about this later.

Once these sugars are absorbed into the bloodstream, they pass by the pancreas, which notifies the cells of the body via a hormone called *insulin* that they need to absorb the sugar from the blood. The amount of insulin produced and released depends upon two things: the amount of sugar ingested and, more importantly, how rapidly it is absorbed into the bloodstream from the gut. The rate at which our blood sugar rises and the effect a food has on insulin production is known as the *glycemic index* of food.

If we eat a high sugar snack all by itself—like a cola and a candy bar—then our blood sugar level rises very quickly. If we eat the same cola and candy bar with some broccoli and Metamucil, then our blood sugar will rise more slowly because the fiber slows the absorption. Likewise, if we eat the same sugary snack with two tablespoons of lard (or a donut), the fat will also delay the absorption. So the effect of a given amount of sugar on your body varies according to what you eat with it. Both fiber and fat slow the absorption of sugar. Protein also has this effect. This is an important principle that, when applied, will help you achieve a balanced diet.

CARBOHYDRATES ARE BROKEN DOWN IN THE BODY INTO THREE MAIN SUGARS:

glucose: *the most common is derived from table sugar, potatoes, corn, rice, pasta and flour.*

fructose: *from table sugar, fruit and fruit juices.*

galactose: *from milk*

UNDERSTANDING **THE IMPORTANT ROLE OF INSULIN**

Insulin's primary job is to pull energy out of the blood. It prevents accumulation that leads to things like dehydration or much worse, falling into a coma. It does this by signaling the cells in our body to take the glucose out of our bloodstream and into the cells. It also tells the liver to quit making glucose. Its goal is to maintain the balance of energy within the blood in a narrowly defined range. You may not realize it but your liver makes up to half of the glucose your body needs every day. This helps explain why you may go to bed with a lower blood sugar level than the one you wake up with in the morning.

Our body begins to experience problems when our fat cells and other cells become resistant to taking in energy from the bloodstream. This is called *insulin resistance syndrome* (IRS). As we discussed earlier, this begins at a BMI of around 25 - 27 and intensifies with weight gain. At this pivotal point, an internal conflict between the bloodstream and the cells begins. They argue over what to do with the excess energy. In response to the failure of the glucose levels to drop, the pancreas makes more insulin, which pushes the cells harder, which leads to increased stress (and inflammation), which drives the development of diabetes, heart attacks, and strokes.

Once this situation has gone on for years, the pancreas begins to fail. This leads to a second problem: low blood sugars, or hypoglycemia, three to four hours after eating. In a normal pancreas, a bolus of insulin is released right after eating to bring down the blood sugar. When the pancreas begins to fail, it releases *less* insulin initially, but then it has to produce more insulin over the next 2 hours or so. In this situation, the extra insulin causes the person's blood sugar level to drop too low three to four hours after eating. Symptoms of hypoglycemia include feeling dizzy, weak, nauseated, shaky, and even confused. The brain detects this change because it is dependent on glucose for energy. Immediately, the brain sends out a message that it needs food. This prompts the person to eat another snack, which is often high in carbohydrates. This keeps the roller coaster ride of sugar highs and lows going.

Insulin's primary job is to signal your cells to take energy out of the blood. The amount of insulin your body produces depends upon the amount of sugar you ingest. Elevated insulin levels are connected with increased rates of diabetes, heart attacks, and strokes.

Millions of Americans ride this ride every day. I did myself many years ago, and I can tell you that it is not very amusing. I used to start my day by eating a high-carbohydrate breakfast that usually consisted of a bowl of cereal and a piece of white toast, a roll or a muffin. By eating a high-carbohydrate, low-protein breakfast, I set myself up for the need to snack throughout the day. I still remember my 10 a.m. "cookie runs" and my afternoon candy bar and cola breaks. As I mentioned earlier, this was a major problem for me and it accounted for a lot of my weight gain.

A group of doctors in Boston did a study a few years ago on the effects of eating a high-carb-only breakfast. They fed a select group of children a high-carbohydrate breakfast, which means it had a high glycemic index and was quickly absorbed into the bloodstream. For the next twenty-four hours, the doctors monitored how much the children ate. They then changed the children's diet by substituting protein for a portion of the high-carbohydrate breakfast. This lowered the glycemic index, thereby decreasing the rate at which the sugar was absorbed into the bloodstream. The effect was obvious. The children ate less and took in fewer calories the following day.

The moral of the story and the rule of thumb we should all follow is clear: A balanced diet that includes carbohydrates, protein and healthy fat will produce a more satisfied appetite. This will lead to less food consumption and give our pancreas some rest. The daily recommended balanced diet includes 40 to 55 percent high-quality carbohydrates, 20 to 30 percent fat and about 20 percent protein. Oh, and don't forget 25 to 30 grams of fiber. Your body will thank you for it!

If you take in fewer carbohydrate- and sugar-laden snacks, you will often consume fewer calories in a day. A balanced diet of 40 to 55 percent high-quality carbohydrates, 20 to 30 percent healthy fat and about 20 percent protein will lead to a more satisfied appetite and less food consumption.

EATING CANDY IS **NOT SUCH A SWEET IDEA**

Let's take what we've learned so far and apply it to a typical vending machine snack. Look at the label from a bag of M&M's. As you can see, it contains 236 calories, which will take roughly 4,720 steps for the average woman to walk off. The label also shows that it has 10 grams of fat, and while some of it is the less dangerous monounsaturated fat, it also has a lot of saturated fat, which is worrisome.

Under carbohydrates, we see three things. First, it lists the amount of dietary fiber. Amazingly, M&M's have fiber—albeit only 1.2 grams. The average American eats about 12 to 18 grams of fiber per day according to the United States National Academy of Sciences, Institute of Medicine. The daily recommendation is 25 to 30 grams. We would have to eat a lot of M&M's to take in that amount of fiber! Better sources of fiber include fresh fruit and vegetables, whole-grain bread, brown rice, soybeans, and legumes like beans and lentils.

M&M's Nutrition Facts

Serving Size: 1.69 oz pkg (69 pcs)
Serving Per Container 1

Amount Per Serving	
Calories 236	Calories from Fat 91
	% Daily Value
Total Fat 10.1 g	0%
Saturated Fat 6.3 g	0%
Monosaturated fat 3.3 g	
Polynsaturated Fat 0.3 g	
Cholesterol 7 mg	
Sodium 29 mg	
Total Carbohydrate 34.2 g	
Dietary Fiber 1.2 g	
Sugars 26 g	
Protein 2.1 g	

Next, notice that the sugar content is 26 grams. This is about 8½ teaspoons—an amount that will definitely do a number on your pancreas and on your blood sugar level if you are diabetic. As a general rule, I try to avoid foods that have more than 10 grams of sugar per serving. Although impossible to do at times, it's a worthy goal.

Finally, notice that the *total carbohydrates* is 34.2 grams. This is 9 grams more than the sum of fiber and sugar. Usually a difference like this is attributed to some form of starch. In this case, however, the hidden source of sugar is corn syrup, a particularly troubling form of carbohydrate that not only raises the blood sugar level but also the triglyceride level. It increases the likelihood of the LDL in your blood forming plaque. Again, this is the really dangerous situation we've talked about that leads to strokes and heart attacks.

The average American eats about 12 to 18 grams of fiber per day. The daily recommendation is 25 to 30 grams. Fiber not only slows the release of sugar into the bloodstream, it also cleans the cracks and crevices of the large and small intestines, removing toxic bacteria that cause disease.

That being said, it is important to calculate the non-fiber carbohydrates in the foods we eat. To do this, simply take the total carbohydrates and subtract the amount of fiber. The higher the amount of non-fiber carbs, the less likely we should eat it. Once we start watching and learning the numbers, it becomes evident that the best carbohydrates are those that are more complex. These include foods like fresh fruits and vegetables, brown rice, sweet potatoes, and whole-grain breads and pastas. An average banana and apple each have about 5 grams of fiber, and good 100 percent whole-grain bread has about 2 to 4 grams of fiber per slice.

Keep in mind, the total amount of calories we want to get from carbohydrates is 40 to 55 percent. On a 1,500-calorie diet, that is 600 to 825 calories from carbohydrates, which equals 150 to 206.25 grams per day. Since there are 4 calories in each gram of carbohydrate, we divide the 600 to 825 calories by 4 to get the total number of grams of carbohydrates to aim for daily.

To put all this in perspective, a bag of M&M's has 34.2 grams of carbohydrates, and a twenty-ounce cola has 60 grams. Combined as a mid-morning snack, these two items together pack 94 grams of carbs, which is about half of our daily total. One bag of M&M's and a cola would require 9,720 steps to undo! That is definitely something to chew on. Remember, it is always better to prevent a problem than to try and undo one after you have it.

The total number of calories from carbohydrates we should consume in a day is 40 to 55 percent. This means if we are eating a 2,000-calorie diet, we should take in no more than 800 to 1,100 calories of carbs. This equals about 200 to 275 grams. Total Carbs = Fiber + Non-fiber Carbohydrates.

WAYS IN WHICH **YOUR BLOOD IS TESTED AND DIAGNOSED**

Figuring out how our body is handling sugar can be a little tricky. It does an amazing, meticulous job of keeping things under control. Therefore, in order to accurately determine its ability to process sugar, our blood sugar level must be checked both before meals and two hours after the initiation of a meal. This is called the pre-prandial reading and the post-prandial reading, and it is done with a glucometer.

If you check your blood sugar before a meal, it will be normal (<100), unless you are already a diabetic. The first sign that your body is having difficulty controlling sugar levels will be an increase in the amount of insulin in your bloodstream. Your insulin level can be measured directly (before eating) or as a blood test called the c-peptide (also before eating), which we will talk more about in just a bit.

If your body continues to lose the ability to process sugar and your pancreas becomes fatigued, the next change will be a rise in the *after-meal* blood sugar level to above 140 mg/dl at two hours. Next, if stress from Unacceptable Sugar and excessive fat in your system continues, your *before-meal* (fasting) blood sugar level will begin to rise above normal, but this will be months to years after the *after-meal* rise occurs.

THE GLUCOSE TOLERANCE TEST

To test your body's ability to handle sugar, your doctor will probably have you drink a bottle of glucose water that contains 75 grams of glucose. He will then check your blood sugar two hours later. This is called the *glucose tolerance test*. It gives you an idea of how well your pancreas can deal with a sugar load. If it is producing the right amount of insulin, you will have a normal blood sugar level after two hours. You could actually do this test at home. Simply drink a 20-ounce cola, wait a couple of hours, and then check your blood sugar level using a glucometer, or glucose monitor. You can borrow one from a friend who has diabetes or purchase one at almost all pharmacies. It's not a perfect test, but it will give you an idea of how your pancreas is working.[5]

The results from a glucose tolerance test will be one of the following diagnoses:

Normal Fasting Glucose and Response

A person is said to have a normal glucose when the fasting glucose is <100. A normal response is when the 2-hour glucose level is less than or equal to **140 mg/dL**.

Impaired Fasting Glucose

When a person has a fasting (before meal) glucose equal to or *greater than* 100 mg/dL and less than 126 mg/dL, they are said to have *impaired fasting glucose*. This is considered a risk factor for developing diabetes in the future. A person with this diagnosis is not labeled a diabetic, but they will probably be tested again in the near future.

Impaired Glucose Tolerance

A person is said to have *impaired glucose tolerance* when the 2-hour glucose results from the oral glucose tolerance test are *greater than or equal to* 140 mg/dL but less than 200 mg/dL. This is also considered a risk factor for developing diabetes in the future.

---

5 http://www.endocrineweb.com/conditions/diabetes/diagnosing-diabetes

Diabetes

A person has diabetes when the fasting glucose is above 125 or the oral glucose tolerance test shows the blood glucose level after 2 hours is *equal to or more than* **200 mg/dL**. These results must be confirmed by a second test on another day.

Both *Impaired Fasting Glucose* and *Impaired Glucose Tolerance* diagnoses are associated with low HDL (good) cholesterol, high triglycerides, high blood pressure and obesity—especially abdominal or visceral obesity. Moreover, regarding both the *Impaired Glucose Tolerance* and *Diabetes* diagnoses, there has recently been discussion about lowering the upper value to 180 mg/dL. This would enable more people to be diagnosed with mild diabetes and allow earlier intervention and hopefully prevention of diabetic complications.

BLOOD SUGAR DIAGNOSIS	AMOUNT OF SUGAR IN BLOOD
Normal Fasting Glucose	Less than or equal to 100 mg/dL
Impaired Fasting Glucose	Greater than 100 mg/dL and less than 126 mg/dL
Impaired Glucose Tolerance	Greater than or equal to 140 mg/dL but less than 200 mg/dL
Diabetes	Equal to or more than 200 mg/dL on two separate occasions

THE C-PEPTIDE OR SERUM INSULIN

As I mentioned, the first sign that your body is having difficulty controlling sugar levels will be an increase in your insulin or c-peptide level. The blood test conducted to follow the rate of insulin production in your body is called a *serum insulin* or *c-peptide level*. After an 8 to 12 hour fast, before eating any food, the amount of insulin in the blood is measured. This gives a good idea of how hard your pancreas has to work to keep your blood sugar controlled. The exact values for this test are a little sketchy, but most clinicians use a blood insulin level of less than 10 as normal. This is equivalent to a c-peptide level of 1.8. If the blood insulin level is greater than 20, there is a significant stress being placed on the system. This is a c-peptide level of over 3.

Let me try to put this in perspective. Let's say a normal c-peptide reading of 1.8 and a blood insulin level of 5 is equivalent to an 8-hour workday for an adult. How long do you think you would last if you were working 16 hours a day straight? A c-peptide level of 3.6 and blood insulin level of 10 to 14 are equivalent to a 16-hour workday. How long do you think you would last if you had to work 24 hours a day? That is what a c-peptide reading of 5.4 and blood insulin level of 15 are equivalent to.

The amazing thing is, our pancreas will often keep going for 5, 10, or even 15 years before it burns out and a person develops diabetes. Strangely, there are some people whose pancreas works this hard and it *never* burns out—they never get diabetes. Unfortunately, what these individuals do acquire is heart disease and strokes. Hopefully you are getting the picture. Unacceptable Sugar levels lead to an internally (metabolically) stressed body and debilitating disease—a place you don't want to go.

C-PEPTIDE LEVEL	INSULIN LEVEL	HOURS OF WORK EQUIVALENT
1.8 = Normal	**5 = Normal**	**8 hours of work**
3.6	**10 to 14**	**16 hours of work**
5.4	**15 or more**	**24 hours of work**

THE PREDX TEST

Since 2009, a new test has become available for the diagnosis of diabetes called the PreDx test. This very sophisticated test looks into several different mechanisms that lead to the development of diabetes. As I mentioned, how well the pancreas can function is one of the key components, but there are a few other factors. The PreDx test also considers how well the fat cells in the body are operating along with the level of inflammation. These are vital to the process. The PreDx test measures these markers in your body, feeds the data into a system, and then calculates the 5-year risk of you developing diabetes. This is in light of data collected over the last 20 years on large populations of patients. The computer then provides you with a number on a scale from 1 to 10 that is proportionate to you developing diabetes.[6]

WHEN ALL ELSE FAILS, **LOOK IN THE MIRROR**

One of the quickest ways I have found to determine what is going on inside your body is to take a good look at yourself in the mirror. Now, I'm not talking about looking at your face. I'm talking about looking at yourself in a full-length mirror without any clothes on before or after your shower. Just stand naked sideways and look at yourself. What do you see? Where are you storing your fat?

In the *presence* of high insulin levels, our body tends to store fat in our stomach, creating the so-called "beer belly." It also gives us an **apple**-shaped appearance. The bigger your belly bulges, the more likely you have a similar bulge of plaque inside your arteries. This is the immediate predecessor of a heart attack or stroke. If your fat is in your belly, watch out. It is more than likely a sign that you are overindulging in sugar. This includes foods such as bread, rice, pasta, potatoes, corn, cookies, cakes, candies, chips, pies, soft drinks, or beer, which contains maltose—another form of sugar.

In the *absence* of high insulin, especially in women, excess fat migrates more to the hips and buttocks, creating a **pear**-shaped appearance. If you

6 http://predictmyrisk.com/

are storing fat in your buttocks and thighs, your insulin level is not as high. However, you are still at risk of experiencing fatigue and joint destruction. If you have both an apple and pear shape, you are storing fat in both areas. You have a significant challenge in front of you, but you can see your situation change once you put your heart and mind to it.

If you look in the mirror and see a large gut, take a look at your diet. You will probably find a lot of processed food like bread, pasta, potatoes, corn, rice, cookies, cakes, candies, chips, beers or colas. Realize that if this is the case, your pancreas is working overtime to produce insulin and remove excess sugar from your bloodstream. Make up your mind to change your menu choices to healthier foods and increase your amount of *Training*. If you don't, the day your pancreas cannot keep up with the pressure of your diet will be the day you become a diabetic. So don't wait! Get out there and shrink that gut!

APPEARANCE IN MIRROR	YOU'RE STORING FAT IN	THIS INDICATES
Apple-shaped	Stomach/Belly	High insulin / c-peptide levels
Pear-shaped	Hips & Buttocks	Low insulin / c-peptide levels but too many calories
Apple- and Pear-shaped	Belly, Hips & Buttocks	High insulin / c-peptide levels and too many calories

IT IS **NEVER TOO LATE**

In 2001, a group of Finnish doctors underwent a landmark study, publishing their findings in the New England Journal of Medicine. They took two groups of people who were at high risk for diabetes and looked at the effects of lifestyle changes. One group went on just as they had before, receiving no special intervention. The second group underwent a lifestyle and counseling program, receiving help from a dietician every two months for four years. At the end of four years the group that had gone to the lifestyle training had a 58 percent reduction in the development of diabetes. Once again, this proves that it is never too late to make changes![7]

UNACCEPTABLE SUGAR:
PRESSING TOWARD THE GOAL

	UNHEALTHY	IMPROVING	ACHIEVING EXCELLENCE
Daily Sugar Intake	Greater than 125 grams	Between 100 to 125 grams	Less than 100 grams

7 J Am Soc Nephrol 14:S108-S113, 2003

PLAYING THE GAME OF HEALTH

5 STEPS TO ELIMINATING UNACCEPTABLE SUGAR

AWARENESS: Are you aware of your blood sugar level? Do you eat foods that are likely to raise or lower it? How often do you eat bread, pasta, corn, potatoes, rice, cookies, cakes, chips, pies, or ice cream? How much soda or beer do you drink per week? Look in the mirror and assess your body shape. Are you an apple or a pear? If you do not know your blood sugar level, take the steps needed to find out.

UNDERSTANDING: Are you seeing and grasping the dangerous health risks of eating too much sugar? Can you see how many of the carbs you eat affect your body in the same way as sugar? What is the most eye-opening information that motivates you to monitor your sugar intake?

HABITS: What are your top three favorite sugary foods or carbs? Are you reading labels to see how many carbohydrates are in the food you eat? When do you reach for these most? Is it when you are stressed or watching TV? Who do you eat them with? How do you feel afterward? Name three things you can do to help you reduce your sugar intake.

ACCOUNTABILITY: Look for others who are trying to alter their carbohydrate or sugar intake. Keep a food journal and agree to share it with your accountability partner. Consider going to a dietitian and reviewing one week's worth of food choices every month or two. Work with others to find healthy food alternatives and share what you find. Play the game of going to the supermarket and researching the top 10 foods you eat. Then look for better choices. If you change 3 or 4, you will make a significant change in your life. Share what you learn with a trusted friend and ask them if you can call them anytime you are being tempted to eat something harmful.

SHARING: Write your victories down in your health journal. From time to time, look back and take note of how often you were victorious over your cravings. Reward yourself for a job well done and look for others who are open to learning about Unacceptable Sugars.

NUMBER FIVE

"Two numbers used to describe blood pressure: systolic pressure and diastolic pressure. The systolic pressure, which is always higher and listed first, measures the force that blood exerts on the arterial walls as the heart pumps blood through the body's cardiovascular system. The diastolic pressure, which is always lower and called out second, is the measurement of force as the heart relaxes to allow blood to flow back into the heart. ...Blood pressure often decreases when weight decreases, and the greater the weight loss, the greater the reduction in blood pressure."

—Jordan Rubin

Jordan Rubin, *Perfect Weight* (Lake Mary, FL: Siloam, A Strang Company, 2008) pp. 208-209.

BLOOD PRESSURE

The **B** in our TROUBLE Assessment stands for *Blood Pressure*. It is the measure of the force at which our blood flows through our arteries. Knowing this number is a major key to knowing if there is any TROUBLE lurking within.

Our blood vessels play a major role in keeping us functioning properly. They make up the transportation system of our body and consist of a series of pipes that carry oxygen, food, messages, and waste products to and from each cell. Every twenty-three seconds, five to six quarts of blood circulate from the heart to the tissues of the body and back. The oxygen, glucose and other nutrients carried in these channels are the lifeblood every cell needs to live. Without these nutrients, our cells would die in a matter of minutes.

Blood vessels are divided into two major categories: the **arterial** system and the **venous** system. Arteries lead *from* the heart to the cells, carrying life-giving oxygen and nutrients. Veins run from the cells back to the heart, returning waste products such as carbon dioxide and acids. The force necessary to push the blood to the cells far exceeds the force needed to return it to the heart. Thus, the walls of the arterial system are much stronger and thicker to withstand the force of each heartbeat.

The force at which the blood flows through the blood vessels is called Blood Pressure. We measure this pressure by wrapping the arm with an inflatable cuff and seeing how much force the heart generates with each beat. The pressure it exerts when it fully contracts is called the *systolic* blood pressure. The pressure it generates when it relaxes is called the *diastolic* blood pressure. The way we express a person's blood pressure is systolic over the diastolic. Blood Pressure (BP) = Systolic pressure/Diastolic pressure = SBP/DBP.

The immediate relaxation of the blood vessels after the heart contracts reinforces the teamwork that occurs between the heart and the blood vessels. This allows blood to flow into the arteries with less resistance. As we age, our arteries become less flexible, and plaque often is deposited in them. This leads to arteries becoming stiff and less able to relax. As this happens, the systolic blood pressure slowly rises. So the increase of plaque and aging of the arteries leads to an increase in blood pressure.

The blood vessels are the transportation system of the body. As the heart contracts, it pushes blood through the arterial system and into the body. Arteries carry nutrient-rich blood from the heart to the cells of the body. Five to six quarts of blood circulate from our heart to our cells and back every twenty-three seconds.

UNDERSTANDING **THE DANGER OF HIGH BLOOD PRESSURE**

Okay...so what is a healthy, normal blood pressure? It is about 115 systolic over 75 diastolic—115/75. Modern studies have shown that the high elevation of the *top* number and the difference between the top and the bottom number (the pulse pressure) are the best predictors of having a heart attack or stroke in people *over* age 50. On the other hand, the high elevation of the bottom number is the most important predictor for people *under* age 50.

The normal heart rate is 60 to 80 beats per minute. People who have 80 to 120 beats per minute are headed for trouble, and those who are experiencing over 120 beats per minute definitely have a problem. For every 20/10 point increase over the normal pressure of 115/75, the chance of having a heart attack or stroke *doubles*. If my patients have a Blood Pressure under 120/80, I am fine with it. If it is greater than 140 over 90, they have high blood pressure or hypertension and I start treating it with medicine.

When the systolic, or top, number goes up, it causes an increase in the force of blood flow in our tender, sensitive tissues, such as our brain and kidneys. This leads to damage of the blood vessels and/or the tissues themselves. Plaque may begin to build up or the blood vessel wall may thicken or hypertrophy. In the brain, this leads to *multi-infarct dementia*, which means a person has multiple small strokes because of inadequate blood flow to areas of the brain. In the kidneys, this leads to renal failure and eventually the need for dialysis. Overall, an increase in blood pressure results in a decrease in functioning and ultimately death of cells and tissue.

Another potential problem from a weakened arterial wall is that it may stretch and ultimately rip under the increased pressure. This is called an *aneurysm*. One of my patients, an executive for a large Fortune 100 firm, came to my office one day complaining of back pain. I did an exam and found no obvious problem. He had no sign of a pulled muscle or kidney stone and no significant arthritis or stomach problems. But over the course of a few days, the pain worsened. Not wanting to take any chances, we got a CAT scan of his abdomen to see what was going on. When the results came, we had our answer. The largest blood vessel in the body, the aorta, was beginning to tear. Although it was not yet critical, it was only a matter of time before it would have ripped open, and he would have died of internal hemorrhaging. That test saved his life!

The sobering fact about high blood pressure is that it is often without symptoms until it is too late. That is, until an "end organ," such as our brain, kidneys or heart, becomes damaged, we rarely feel it. Occasionally, some individuals with high blood pressure get headaches or blurry vision. But usually they ascribe these symptoms to stress or tension. This is how hypertension got the name "the great silent killer." Many times the first sign that the silent killer has invaded our body is when we experience kidney failure, an aneurysm, a stroke or a heart attack.

One of my greatest goals in life is to help people avoid this type of irreversible damage and live the healthy life we were meant to live. Some causes of hypertension are preventable and can be reversed. Certain tumors, kidney problems and heart conditions that lead to blood pressure elevations are correctable once we discover and address the root cause. Therefore, have your doctor look for these other conditions, checking them out with your blood work and any other tests they feel are necessary to reveal these reversible symptoms.

For every 20/10 point increase over the normal pressure of 115/75, the chance of having a heart attack or stroke ***doubles****. If you have high blood pressure, do not ignore it! Hypertension is often called "the great silent killer" because many people often do not feel any pain until it kills them suddenly.*

HOW **SALT EFFECTS BLOOD PRESSURE**

In Texas, we understand the meaning of summer heat. Temperatures often soar over 100, and experiencing days or weeks without rain are not unusual. On hot, sticky nights, all we want is something refreshing to help us cool down and forget the sweltering heat. Some may think, what better summer night drink than a margarita? Well, that is not necessarily the case.

Unfortunately, the amount of salt in a margarita is high. As it is taken in, sodium quickly flows into the bloodstream. To deal with this dilemma, our kidneys retain water to dilute the salt content. Our kidneys are the volume controllers of our blood. Whether it is a margarita or another salt-saturated food, our kidneys are designed to maintain healthy blood-salt content. Having too much sodium in the blood is called *hypernatremia*. This condition leads to mental confusion, heart problems and death to cells.

Most individuals can tolerate an increased amount of sodium from one food item without difficulties. Our blood vessels usually operate half filled. So to accommodate the situation, they just relax and allow the increased volume to work its way through the system, allowing the kidneys to catch up and process the excess salt load. As we age, however, our body's ability to handle excessive amounts of salt diminishes. Our arteries and kidneys don't always work as well as they did when we were younger. They may be able to handle the surplus salt from *one* food item, but any additional salty foods will tip the scales.

Salty foods are often eaten in concert with others. For example, if we are eating a Mexican meal, salsa, chips, enchiladas, and sopapillas are often eaten together—all of which contain copious amounts of salt. If we're eating our favorite combo, the burger, fries and soda are also filled with sodium, not to mention a lot of fat. Excessive amounts of salt in the blood stream cause the blood pressure to rise dramatically. Unfortunately, the body has no warning system for this, so we usually don't feel any symptoms. If we do have symptoms, we often ascribe them to other ingredients in our food or to being tired. Consequently, the real problem goes unnoticed.

High blood pressure resulting from an excessive amount of salt in our diet is a phenomenon that occurs frequently in modern society. As mentioned earlier, almost all of our processed foods contain moderate to large amounts of salt. From potato chips and hot dogs to canned soup and macaroni and cheese, salt is added to enhance flavor and preserve shelf life. We must develop a healthy habit of reading food labels.

For example, check out the food label for a popular processed cheese. As you can see, it packs quite a punch in several areas. It has a high amount of saturated fat—74 of the 101 calories are from fat. It also contains 443 mg of sodium, which is about 25 percent of the daily recommended salt intake. Remember, we want our daily consumption of fat to remain below 30 percent of our total calories, and the amount of salt we consume should be less than 2 grams (2,000 mg). I am *not* saying you can never eat a slice of this cheese. What I am saying is be aware of what you are eating so that you don't overload your system with too much salt or fat. An ounce of prevention is worth a pound of cure.

Excessive amounts of salt in the bloodstream cause our blood pressure to rise dramatically. Our daily consumption of salt should be less than 2 grams (2,000 mg). To know how much sodium you are taking in, read the food labels.

WHAT ABOUT **WEIGHT GAIN**?

Cheese American, Swiss, Processed | Nutrition Facts

Serving Size: 1 oz, Land O' Lakes
Serving Per Container

Amount Per Serving	
Calories 101	Calories from Fat 74
	% Daily Value
Total Fat 8.3 g	0%
Saturated Fat 5.2 g	0%
Monosaturated fat 2.2 g	
Polynsaturated Fat 0.3 g	
Cholesterol 26 mg	
Sodium 443 mg	
Total Carbohydrate 0.7 g	
Dietary Fiber 0 g	
Sugars 0 g	
Protein 5.8 g	

Our blood pressure will also increase as a result of weight gain. There are a number of reasons this occurs. One of the most eye-opening is that our body creates and lays down new blood vessels at the same time our fat cells pack away fat. For every pound of fat we gain, our body manufactures and lays down an additional *mile* of blood vessels and then pump blood the increased distance to keep the tissues alive. Wow!

So, if a person is 30 pounds overweight, they have approximately 30 extra miles of blood vessels to create and pump blood through. Excess weight also makes the heart work harder, which translates to more beats per minute. There are 60 minutes in an hour and 24 hours in a day. If this person's heart beats 80 times a minute, his heart will beat about 115,200 beats a day—that is 80 x 60 x 24. What's more, his heart will have to pump blood an additional 3,456,000 *miles per day! Do the math:* 80 x 60 x 24 x 30 miles.

Current statistics estimate that over two-thirds of all Americans are overweight, a number of which are morbidly obese. There is little wonder why epidemics of both hypertension and congestive heart failure are currently appearing in our country today. It's high time we get into the game and start calling some different plays.

Our body creates and lays down new blood vessels at the same time our fat cells pack away fat. For every pound of fat we gain, our body has to manufacture an additional mile of blood vessels and then pump blood the increased distance to keep the tissues alive.

HOW **SALT EFFECTS BLOOD PRESSURE**

As a first-year medical student, I arrived convinced that modern medicine had all the answers. I believed I was in for the educational experience of a lifetime. When we started pathophysiology, I just knew the teachers were speaking the "gospel" truth regarding the human body. Likewise, with regard to cardiovascular disease, such as strokes, heart attacks, and aneurysms, I was very sure that we in the medical profession had it all figured out. Smoking, diabetes, high blood pressure, elevated cholesterol, lack of exercise, estrogen deficiency, and family history are all factors that lead to a weakened and broken heart…or so I believed.

At some point in my journey I remember wondering: What on earth do these seven things have in common? Why do a lack of estrogen and exercise have the same effect as diabetes and smoking? At that time, I was told that these factors led to a gradual blockage of the blood vessels by an accumulation of plaque—the process known as atherosclerosis. When the opening in the artery became too small for blood to flow through it, a blood clot formed. Any tissues downstream from this clot died, and the person with such a condition would experience a heart attack, stroke or another unexpected, catastrophic event.

While all these things are true to an extent, there are other factors involved that the medical profession was unaware of at the time. The truth is, medical information and understanding doubles about every two years. We are constantly learning new things. What we think is correct today will be modified in the years ahead as our knowledge increases.

One powerful factor determining the health of the heart and the circulatory system we were not aware of in the 1980s is the key role the *vascular endothelium* plays. This thin, one-cell-layer lining of our blood vessels is a pivotal part of the health of our entire body. It was overlooked for decades in the medical field, apparently because of its thinness and suspected frailty. Nevertheless, this seemingly insignificant lining is the largest endocrine gland in the human body!

Altogether it weighs over 1.6 pounds in the average adult male. If we took our skin off and made it into a carpet (strange thought, but stay with me), it would be three feet by three feet square. However, if we took the lining of all our blood vessels and put it together, the vascular endothelium would measure three *football fields* in size! This amazing, microscopic layer sets the stage for health or disease. If it is healthy, the body is positioned to be healthy. If it is damaged, the door is open for disease to develop.

---

*The **vascular endothelium**, the inner lining of all our blood vessels, is the largest endocrine gland in the human body. This seemingly insignificant layer sets the stage for health or disease within the body. If it is healthy, the body is positioned to be healthy. If it is damaged, the door is open for disease to develop.*

WHAT HAPPENS **WHEN THE LINING GETS DAMAGED**?

One of the most common initial irritants to the lining of the blood vessels is the persistent presence of insulin. As we learned earlier, when digested food is making its way through the small intestines, the pancreas releases the hormone insulin. Insulin serves as a messenger that signals the cells of the body to open their doors and let the "food" in. The more sugar and fat we eat, the more insulin is needed to tell the cells to take it in. When the cells are full, excess sugar and fat remain in the blood. This causes the pancreas to produce and release more insulin. Eventually the cells become resistant to insulin, giving way to the *insulin resistance syndrome* (IRS) that we have discussed earlier in this book. This is also known as *metabetes*—the name describing this pre-diabetic condition.

When metabetes moves into the neighborhood, our vascular endothelial lining begins experiencing significant stress. Once it is damaged, a chain reaction of destruction begins. The lining begins to react by sending up "warning flags" called ICAMs (intracellular adhesion molecules) or VCAMs (vascular adhesion molecules). These fighter molecules sound an alarm for the "law enforcement" of the body to come and make repairs to the damaged lining.

The "law" arrives in the form of molecules called macrophages. Their job is to absorb the excess LDL, or lethal cholesterol, and protect the blood vessel from plaque formation. However, because there is not enough room in the blood vessel for both the macrophage and LDL molecules, further irritation occurs. This releases more ICAMs and VCAMS that call for help. More macrophages come to the scene and another battle ensues. This vicious cycle of irritation or inflammation with the LDL molecules and the macrophage cells causes the wall of the artery to become "hot" from the conflict.

From here, one of two things will happen. The body will get relief from the fight because we get up and start exercising and making changes to our eating habits or we begin to take cholesterol- lowering medication. If these positive adjustments are not made, a life-threatening consequence will ensue. The combination of LDL and macrophage molecules become intertwined and burrowed into the artery wall as "foam cells," the primary ingredient in plaque. This plaque may become unstable and rupture into the bloodstream. This results in "exploding plaque," the underlying cause of both heart attacks and strokes.

Other things that damage the lining of blood vessels include high blood pressure, diabetes, smoking, a persistent amount of emotional stress or depression, and excess fat/cholesterol in the blood. Sadly, any one of these problems by themselves is dangerous. However, when two or more are present working together, they become a lethal wrecking crew. Instead of just attacking one area of the body, they bring destruction to multiple areas—attacking arteries in places like the legs, kidneys, neck, and head simultaneously. The only thing worse than being in trouble with the "IRS" (having Insulin Resistance Syndrome) is being in TROUBLE and not being able to do anything about it.

High blood pressure, diabetes, smoking, persistent amounts of insulin or emotional stress hormones in the bloodstream, and excess fat/cholesterol in the blood damage the lining of blood vessels. Sadly, any one of these problems by themselves is dangerous. However, when two or more are present working together, they become a lethal wrecking crew.

THE **THREADBARE TIRE PRINCIPLE**

As a student at Tampa General Hospital, I spent a lot of time in the medicine wards and in the emergency room. One month, while working in the ER, a very nice, older African-American patient, who I'll call "Henry," came in with a prostate problem. While treating him, I noticed his blood pressure was high. I asked him if he had ever been told this. He looked at his wife and daughter who were in the room and chuckled, "Yes, they tell me that, but I never had any trouble with it, so I don't treat it." I insisted on writing him a prescription for high blood pressure medicine and asked his family to make sure he took it. People of all ethnicities have an increase in blood pressure as they age. But African-Americans have a greater risk. In fact, by the time African-American women are 80 years old, 80 percent of them have blood pressures of over 140/90.

Several months later, when I was on the intensive care unit (ICU) rotation, Henry came back to the hospital, only this time it was because of a stroke. Because I had seen him and had a relationship with his family, the resident doctor asked me to monitor the case personally through the night.

That was one of the most devastating nights of my life. We tried to control Henry's blood pressure with intravenous drips. Unfortunately, part of his brain was not getting blood, and it was dying. The part of his body it controlled was moving uncontrollably. About halfway through the night, his brain began to swell and push its way through the opening in his supporting tissue inside the skull. His arms and legs then stretched out and assumed a position we call decorticate posturing. Soon afterward, he began to have seizures, and finally, he died. His wife just kept crying and saying, "He never would take his medicine." I did my best to ease her conscience, but we both knew this could have been prevented.

As a doctor, one of the most frustrating things to deal with is a patient who refuses to take his/her medicine. Years ago, when I diagnosed my patients with high cholesterol, I would immediately ask them to begin therapy. However, only four out of ten would agree to it. When asked why, they often responded, "I feel just fine. It can't be that big of a deal."

I tried to politely explain the seriousness of their situation, but it rarely did any good. Finally, in my desperation to wake people up, I began saying, "It doesn't matter how you feel. This condition will still kill you." This increased my success rate somewhat, but it still wasn't what it should be. And a number of my patients mistook my sense of urgency for rudeness and insensitivity. So I began to use the following analogy:

A man pulled off a highway into a filling station to fuel up his pristine 1970 Ford pickup. The attendant saw him pull in and struck up a conversation.

"Nice old truck you've got there," the attendant commented.

"Yup," replied the man proudly, "I been driving it for a lot of years."

As they spoke the attendant noticed the tires were all completely bald.

"Uh...change your tires recently?" he asked with raised eyebrows.

"Nope, never. And do ya know what? I've got over 100,000 miles on this truck, and it drives great and ain't never had a flat."

At this point, more of my patients began to get the idea. My success rate of getting them to take their medication and do therapy increased to about seven out of ten. I guess the others will have to experience a "blowout" to take it seriously. Hopefully you are not one of them. It takes a mature person to feel fine, yet pay money for medication, doctor visits, lab tests, and deal with the inconvenience of it all based upon someone encouraging them to do it. Hopefully, as you play the Game of Health and understand what is actually happening in your body, the motivation to stay in the Game and win will become easier and more likely to occur.

People of all ethnicities have an increase in blood pressure as they age. But African-Americans have a greater risk. In fact, by the time African-American women are 80 years old, 80 percent of them have blood pressures of over 140/90.

IT'S TIME TO **TAKE ACTION NOW**!

So what is your *Blood Pressure*? If you don't know, it is time to find out. If you *do* know your blood pressure and it is higher than it should be, there is no time like the present to take action. The same is true if you have elevated Oil or Unacceptable Sugar levels.

The "Seventh Report of the Joint National Committee on Prevention, Detection, Evaluation, and Treatment of High Blood Pressure" provides guidelines for hypertension prevention and management. Here are its key findings:

> In people **over 50**, *systolic blood pressure* greater than 140 mmHg is a much more important cardiovascular disease (CVD) risk factor than diastolic blood pressure.
>
> The risk of developing CVD doubles with each increment of 20/10 mmHg beyond the healthy pressure of 115/75 mmHg. Individuals who have a normal blood pressure at age 55 have a *90 percent* lifetime risk for developing hypertension.
>
> Individuals with a systolic blood pressure of 120–139 mmHg or a diastolic blood pressure of 80–89 mmHg should be considered pre-hypertensive and require health-promoting lifestyle modifications to prevent the development of heart attacks and strokes.[8]

Without a doubt, the human body is incredibly created and very accommodating. It's always trying to adapt and adjust to whatever we eat, drink and do. It will bend over backwards to keep us functioning properly. So take some time to learn more about your body and give it what it needs. By lowering your blood pressure through increased exercise, salt restriction, and medication if need be, you can get your numbers where they need to

7 J Am Soc Nephrol 14:S108-S113, 2003

be and maximize your chances of avoiding "stiff vessels" and reverse the process of plaque buildup, and in many cases, prevent the progression into irreversible consequences. Get with your healthcare provider. See where you are in the Game, and team up to send hypertension back to its bench. Yes, it may require some effort and be a bit inconvenient, but it will make a big difference in the quality and length of your life.

BLOOD PRESSURE: PRESSING TOWARD THE GOAL

	UNHEALTHY	IMPROVING	ACHIEVING EXCELLENCE
Systolic	Greater than 140	Between 120 to 140	Less than 120
Diastolic	Greater than 90	Between 80 to 90	Less than 80

5 STEPS TO IMPROVING YOUR BLOOD PRESSURE

AWARENESS: What is your blood pressure? Is it normal, borderline, or high? Is it where you would like it to be? Are you in TROUBLE?

UNDERSTANDING: From this chapter, can you see the chain reaction of problems that arise as a result of high blood pressure? Do you see how not dealing with it will eventually not only affect you but those whom you love? What steps can you take to either lower your blood pressure if it's high or maintain a healthy blood pressure?

HABITS: Blood pressure can be greatly affected by sodium (salt) intake, your level of fitness (especially aerobic fitness) and your weight. Are you in the habit of looking at labels to check the salt content? Do you get your heart rate to your goal level for at least 20 minutes 3 times weekly? Is your BMI at goal? What habits are keeping these three keys from getting to goal?

ACCOUNTABILITY: Who prepares your food? Can you team up with them to cut sodium? How about aerobic exercise? Who could you ask to work out with you and help you stay in shape? Is there a group at church, work or school that may be helpful to keep you on track? What is your goal? Who can you declare it to and have them ask you regularly if you are meeting it? It takes a village to live a great life. Don't try to do it alone!

SHARING: As you become more and more disciplined in your training and eating regimen, record your blood pressure every time you have it taken. Write it down in your journal. Look back after a few months and see how much you've been able to lower it. Reward yourself for sticking to your plan and getting healthy! Do something you have wanted to do for a long time but have not gotten around to. Who can you share this life-changing information with?

NUMBER SIX

"Every year in the U.S. over 392,000 people die from tobacco-caused disease, making it the leading cause of preventable death. Another 50,000 people die from exposure to secondhand smoke. Tragically, each day thousands of kids still pick up a cigarette for the first time. The cycle of addiction, illness and death continues. …Quitting smoking is the single most important step a smoker can take to improve the length and quality of his or her life."

—American Lung Association

Retrieved 5/18/11 (http://www.lungusa.org/stop-smoking/ and http://www.lungusa.org/stop-smoking/how-to-quit/getting-help/).

LOUSY HABITS

The **L** in our TROUBLE Assessment stands for *Lousy Habits*. A habit is a behavior pattern developed by frequent repetition. It is closely connected with both the way we think and how we feel emotionally. *Lousy Habits* rob us of a quality life and in some cases, shorten our years. They compound the negative effects of unhealthy food choices, increased Roundness and a lack of Training in our lives.

There are countless Lousy Habits we can develop, ranging from taking drugs and drinking excessive amounts of alcohol to watching too much TV and not getting enough sleep. But there is one Lousy Habit I want to zero in on—one that has impacted the lives of almost all of us directly or indirectly. That is the Lousy Habit of *smoking*.

THE **DESTRUCTIVE PROPERTIES OF CIGARETTES**

What do you think of when you see a cigarette? Picture this: Tobacco seeds are planted and the ground is fertilized with chemicals. As the plants grow, they are sprayed with pesticides. Once tobacco leaves fully mature, they are picked and transported to a factory where they are soaked in preservatives and other flavorings. They are then packaged into neat, small cigarettes for distribution. We now know that addictive-forming ingredients are added to cigarettes. This means the entire manufacturing process is carefully manipulated to insure that the smoker's "experience" is carefully controlled and keeps them coming back for more.

All of us have heard of the straw that broke the camel's back. Well, tobacco is the match that ignites the fire inside a person's blood vessels. This is especially true when they already have their hands full dealing with the "IRS"—Insulin Resistance Syndrome, or metabetes. In this condition, smoking irritates the "silver lining" of our blood vessels, the vascular endothelium, even more. As a result, its healthy functioning declines even further.

When a person lights up and inhales, all that was put into making the cigarette is breathed into the lungs. I call these the "products of ignition." They include the fertilizers, pesticides, preservatives, flavorings, burned paper, and of course, nicotine. There are actually over 200 different chemicals found in cigarettes, including arsenic, carbon monoxide, miscellaneous hydrocarbons, and other free radicals and toxins. All of these are heated to red-hot temperatures, inhaled into the lungs, transferred to the blood and dispersed throughout the body.

Smoking unleashes an attack of literally tens of thousands of destructive energy particles within the body. As they make their way through the bloodstream, dangerous free radicals strike and injure the walls of the arteries. These new open wounds become gaps for lethal LDL cholesterol to sneak in and lodge within the blood vessel wall. The inflammation and irritation LDL brings leads to a damaged artery, which is the first step in the accumulation of plaque, which we will see in the next chapter.

Sadly, each cigarette will take five to seven minutes off a smoker's life. Death comes an average of 15 years earlier for a smoker than a non-smoker. Clearly, lighting up is a Lousy Habit that leaves a lousy legacy for generations to come.

Addiction-forming ingredients are added to cigarettes. Over 200 different chemicals are found in them, including arsenic, carbon monoxide, hydrocarbons, and other free radicals and toxins. Each cigarette will take five to seven minutes off a smoker's life. Death comes an average of 15 years earlier for a smoker than a non-smoker.

MY EXPERIENCE **WORKING WITH SMOKERS**

The use of cigarettes and other nicotine-based products is one of the most perplexing trends we have in the U.S. today. As a medical student at the Tampa Veterans Administration Hospital, I saw the tragic result of our government's discount cigarette program manifested in former soldiers day after day, literally by the hundreds. The story always ends the same. Veterans developed lung cancer, chronic obstructive pulmonary disease (COPD), suffocation from emphysema or plaque formation resulting in a stroke, aneurysm, or heart attack.

As a young, enthusiastic student of the healing arts, it was incomprehensible to me that people could so knowingly kill themselves through smoking. I can remember becoming boiling angry at the patients as they suffered from what I felt was self-induced agony. And God forbid if they complained, because I didn't want to hear it! I simply had no tolerance. At that time I had no *understanding* of the nature of the addiction they suffered from. It just seemed they were reaping what they had sown. I remember saying with great bravado as a first-year med student, "I will not see smokers in *my* practice when I graduate."

The thing that eventually saved me from my ignorance and arrogance was my love of history. As a child, I was a member of the military book club. Yeah, I was a nerd. Nevertheless, I read all of the books by Edward L. Beach, like *Run Silent Run Deep*, and *The Two Ocean War: A Short History of the U.S. Navy in the Second World War* by Samuel Eliot Morison. I basically knew World War II in terms of the battles—what happened and who won.

This love of history peaked during those all-nighters when I was on call in the Veterans Administration Hospital. I often sat in the ward, monitoring patients and conversing with veterans about their war experiences. Several of these men had fought on the beaches of the Pacific Ocean. Some had even been on submarines and survived being sunk! Others were pilots who fought in the European theater, the Pacific theater, or both. The more I talked with them, the more I learned that they were not "bad," irresponsible men. They were the backbone of our military doing their best to protect our freedom during the Second World War.

Forty-three years after the last shots of the war had been fired, they were still experiencing the ravages of battle. The only difference was that the enemy no longer had a face, and death no longer came in the form of gunshots or bomb blasts. These men were now experiencing the consequences of serving in a very scary war—one in which they were not sure if they would live another day. To help the men cope with the stresses of war, our government had provided free and discount cigarettes. Many men shared with amazement their memories of being able to go to the base to buy packs of cigarettes for twenty-five cents.

Cigarette programs were not a malicious or careless act. They were primarily a decision made without the proper medical knowledge. It wasn't until many years after the war that the dangers of smoking were realized. By the mid-1980s, we better understood the destructive nature of cigarettes and that they were killing thousands of our veterans. By then, many veterans and common folk alike had a serious addiction that they could not figure out how to break free from. For many, it was too late to receive much benefit from stopping.

Separating the person from the disease was a hard lesson to learn. It was one of those rights of passage for me as a medical student. Initially, I attempted to assign an explanation to each person for every medical problem they had. I wanted to make them admit that *they* had brought the problems onto themselves. This way I could feel confident that if I did the right things in my own life, I would never experience the same problems. Those long nights on call in the ward did a lot more than teach me medicine. They taught me about life and helped me understand that bad things *do* happen to good people.

For U.S. veterans and common folk alike, smoking cigarettes always creates the same kind of results: lung cancer, chronic obstructive pulmonary disease (COPD), suffocation from emphysema or a stroke, aneurysm or a heart attack.

UNDERSTANDING **HOW ADDICTION TAKES ROOT**

To understand how a person becomes addicted to smoking, we must first understand a few things about nicotine and the human body. Nicotine is a *neurotransmitter*. It is a normal, healthy, important molecule that transmits nerve impulses and messages from one nerve to the next. It is associated with a part of the nervous system that's involved with alertness and focus. The interesting thing is, our body produces nicotine all by itself.

So here we have our poor, unsuspecting young soldier, who we'll call "George." Not knowing if he's going to see the next sunrise, he is offered the "pleasure" of discount cigarettes. He begins smoking, and within a short time, becomes addicted to the nicotine delivery device. If we tested George before and after he smoked, we'd find his test-taking ability was better *after* smoking his cigarette than before.

After George smokes for a few weeks, his body realizes that it no longer needs to make its own nicotine because of the seemingly endless supply of it flowing into the bloodstream from an unknown source. His body then proceeds to tear down its nicotine-producing factories. If George quits smoking, his focus and test-taking abilities will temporarily sink below the level they were before he started smoking. *He has to smoke to get back to his baseline functioning.*

Nicotine is a normal, healthy neurotransmitter—an important molecule that transmits messages from one nerve to the next. It is associated with a part of the nervous system that's involved with alertness and focus. The interesting thing is, our body produces nicotine all by itself.

From this point forward, if George doesn't get his military ration of cigarettes, he will go through physical withdrawals from the absence of nicotine. His body's nervous system needs to send messages, but without its nicotine factories or the external provision of nicotine from smoking, it is unable to do so. It will take at least three days to rebuild its internal factories. During this time George will be irritable, feel jittery, suffer from insomnia and perhaps develop a rapid heartbeat and sweating. He will want a cigarette so desperately that he will go through the ritual of seeking one out. He is now addicted to the neurotransmitter delivery device we know as cigarettes.

Another controlling factor that comes with cigarette smoking is the perceived relaxation it brings. Think about it. When George needs to smoke, he gets up, strolls over to a quiet place, lights up a cigarette and reflects on his day. Unconsciously, he has done a good thing by taking a moment to relax. Unfortunately, he has now attached smoking to relaxation. Now whenever he feels irritable or stressed for any reason, he heads off for a cigarette to calm his nerves. He has established smoking as a way of coping with stress.

In a short time, smoking becomes a *reflex*. If the phone rings, George grabs a cigarette. When he gets into the car to drive to work, he grabs a cigarette. When he gets out of the shower, finishes dinner, goes for a walk, and so forth, he grabs a cigarette. Eventually, lighting up is second nature and requires no thought on his part whatsoever. He has acquired a deeply seated Lousy Habit.

Not all of us are equally susceptible to the addictive power of cigarettes or other tobacco products. This fact becomes especially pronounced when we take a look in the psychiatric wards of hospitals. Seemingly every psychotic person craves cigarettes, as do many of those with a manic-depressive illness. On the other hand, those with obsessive-compulsive disorders and anxiety disorders smoke far less. It has become evident that those individuals who have a psychiatric disorder involving low dopamine levels are more prone to smoke. Consequently, it will be more difficult for them to quit.

If a person quits smoking, it will take at least three days for their body to rebuild its internal nicotine factories. During this time, he will be irritable, feel jittery, suffer from insomnia and perhaps develop a rapid heartbeat and sweating.

TAKING THE **STEPS TO WALK IN FREEDOM**

Thankfully, there are successful ways to quit smoking. Through commitment, perseverance and a good plan, it can be done! To be effective, the plan must address each of the issues mentioned in the previous section. Let's take a look at a proven plan of action based on the five points in the Game of Health.

The first step to freedom is honestly becoming **aware** of your condition. Ask yourself, *Do I have a problem with nicotine? Am I addicted?* If you are and you admit it, you have moved out of the Dugout of Life and are in position to begin making your way around the bases.

Your next step is **understanding**, which means learning about tobacco's effects on your body and the importance of moving beyond the addiction. We already mentioned a number of effects tobacco has, but you can learn even more through the additional resources we have made available online at **www.mysevenhealers.com**.

The greatest key to freedom is dealing with the pure physical addiction to nicotine. Again, the body must have nicotine in order to function. Weaning oneself of smoking in steps through "nicotine replacement therapy" is a proven remedy. This includes the use of nicotine gums, patches or delivery devices like smokeless cigarettes. You may ask, "Well, isn't that just as bad?" In a sense, it is similar to smoking in that it continues to supply nicotine externally. However, it does not deliver the other toxins associated with lighting a cigarette, and the doses of nicotine are carefully controlled and systematically reduced to slowly wean a person off external sources. For instance, nicotine patches can be reduced from 21 mg to 14 mg to 7 mg before eliminating it completely.

If a person chooses to stop smoking cold turkey, their body will rebuild its nicotine factories and begin producing nicotine again after about 72 hours. This period will be more than a little difficult, but some would rather tough it out as opposed to gradually tapering off over days, weeks, or months with gum, patches or smokeless forms of nicotine.

The greatest key to freedom from smoking is dealing with the physical addiction to nicotine. Weaning oneself in steps through "nicotine replacement therapy" is a proven remedy. This includes the use of nicotine gums, patches or delivery devices like smokeless cigarettes.

New ways of managing stress will also be needed to quit. The relaxing break that smoking provides—standing up, walking outside, talking with friends, and taking a few deep breaths is a good form of therapy. To suddenly stop these things can lead to a return to smoking. Harnessing the good habits and eliminating the Lousy Habit of smoking is the key. StressMaps is a tool I use to help patients identify and address the areas of their life in which they are struggling and provide them with tools to overcome them. You can check out StressMaps at **www.thesevennumbers.com**.

Once you are aware of where you are and have a better understanding of your situation, it is time to develop ***new habits***. Experts estimate it takes about 21 days to establish these. New, healthier patterns of behavior will help prevent an inadvertent return to smoking. Some successful habits to consider include wearing a rubber band and flicking it when the urge to smoke returns. Deep-breathing exercises and counting backward from 10 may also be helpful.

I have worked with many people who have quit smoking, and it appears that with each unhealthy habit they have had, they had to "say no" to it *three* times before it was "extinguished." Therefore, if the average person has about 50 different cues to smoke, we will need to say NO about 150 times. Everyday activities such as showering, driving, eating, having sex, and experiencing stressful situations are often triggers to light up. If any of these are triggers for you, you will have to recognize them and guard yourself to do one of the proactive "antidotes" like deep breathing, the rubber band, or some other refocusing technique to move past these cues.

The second to last step in our trip around the bases is establishing **accountability**. Finding trustworthy people who will support us in our endeavors is a major key to victory. Stop and think. Who can be recruited to help you quit smoking? Friends, family members and coworkers can be great accountability partners during the challenging transition. When my dad wanted to kick the habit back in the 60s, my sister and I gladly agreed to act as protagonists in the effort. The key is to find someone who you talk with or see regularly who won't condemn you for falling off the wagon but at the same time won't condone it either.

Sharing is the final step. Once you have gotten the upper hand in the situation, it is time to begin telling others about your success and offer them help with their struggles. They may ask you questions you don't know the answers to, and that's okay. You can simply refer back to your research sources online or in books and find the answer they need. You may also come up with a completely different way to manage the problem—an idea they had not thought of! By being real, transparent, and willing to help others, you will develop a greater level of freedom than you ever thought possible!

New ways of managing stress will also be needed to quit smoking. This means developing new, healthy habits and saying "no" to the old ones. It appears that with each unhealthy habit you have, you will have to say no to it three times before it is "extinguished."

Don't Let Lousy Habits Master You!

There is a powerful saying written about 2,000 years ago, and I believe it is very true. It says, "Everything is permissible (allowable and lawful) for me; but not all things are helpful (good for me to do, expedient and profitable when considered with other things). Everything is lawful for me, but *I will not become the slave of anything* or be brought under its power" (1 Corinthians 6:12 AMP). A Lousy Habit, like smoking, may be permissible, but it is definitely *not* helpful or profitable when considered with other things. In most cases it does enslave the person who practices it.

Don't let *Lousy Habits* master you or rob you of a desirable, quality life. If cigarette smoking is a problem, make a solid decision to break free from it. If it's watching too much TV or not getting enough sleep, develop a plan of action to break free. Consult your doctor and seek help from trusted friends.

Only by acknowledging the problem and addressing it will you truly be free. Don't believe the lie that you can't do it. YOU CAN! You can do anything if you put your heart and mind into it. Live your life one day at a time and look for ways to establish healthy habits. Not only will *you* reap the reward of your choices, but your children and your children's children will too!

LOUSY HABITS:
PRESSING TOWARD THE GOAL

HABITS	UNHEALTHY	IMPROVING	ACHIEVING EXCELLENCE
Smoking/ Tobacco Use	Yes	Yes but less	No
Hours of TV Per Week	20 or more	15 to 20	Less than 15
Hours of Sleep per Week	Less than 49	49 to 54	Greater than 54

PLAYING THE GAME OF HEALTH

5 STEPS TO ELIMINATING THE LOUSY HABIT OF SMOKING

AWARENESS: Do you smoke? If the answer is yes, how often do you smoke and how long have you been smoking?

UNDERSTANDING: Do you understand the deadly effects that smoking has on your body? Although it is hard to quit, can you see why it is vital that you try? Take a piece of paper and draw a line down the center of it. On one side of the line, list some reasons why you'd like to quit smoking. On the other side, list reasons why you don't want to quit. Does the column listing the reasons you want to quit outweigh the column listing the reasons you want to smoke?

HABITS: What habits in your daily routine motivate you to light up? In what practical ways can you change the way you respond to the stimulus to smoke—what healthy habits can you develop to help you relax and deal with stress in a constructive way?

ACCOUNTABILITY: To whom can you be accountable to help you quit smoking? Ask them to ask you how you are doing on a regular basis. Also, check with your doctor to see if he has any resources that will help you in your effort to quit. You may also want to consider joining a support group or coaching program if there is one available.

SHARING: Take time daily to read your list of reasons to quit smoking. Remind yourself regularly why you are giving it up. Record your struggles and triumphs in your health journal. Look over it from time to time to see how much you grow throughout the process. As you gain victory over the urge, look for opportunities to share your story with others.

NUMBER SEVEN

"…Imagine your arteries as being like streets in a city. We use the streets of a city to get from place to place. Similarly, your blood uses the arteries as a means to get from one place to another. It uses the vessels to carry nutrients and oxygen to the cells, and then carry carbon dioxide and other by-products of metabolism away from the cells. But the arteries, just like streets and highways, eventually wear down. They become clogged with fatty buildup called plaque, or narrowed from swelling and inflammation…. The older and more congested arteries get, the more subject they are to blood clots, the body's version of traffic jams."

—Michael F. Roizen, M.D.

Michael F. Roizen, M.D., The RealAge Makeover (New York, NY: HarperCollins Publishers, 2004) p. 93.

EXPLODING PLAQUE

The **E** in our TROUBLE Assessment stands for *Exploding Plaque*. Throughout our journey, I have talked about plaque formation and the problems it brings. In this final section, we want to take a closer look at the reality of what happens to men and women when plaque builds up in the arteries and then ruptures without warning.

UNDERSTANDING **HOW THE BODY RESPONDS TO PLAQUE**

The metabolic war within the bloodstream eventually moves into the walls of our arteries if left unchecked. The lining of the blood vessel, or vascular endothelium, then quits functioning normally. This enables, or encourages, LDL (lousy, lethal cholesterol) and macrophage molecules to invade the wall and pour fuel on an intensifying, fiery battle. As the fight continues, plaque grows. This increases the likelihood of it rupturing and spilling its fatty gel into the bloodstream.

The body, sensing the impending TROUBLE, sends in special "troops" to fight and protect the bloodstream from exposure to the fatty gel and an almost certain blockage of the artery. These troops are *smooth muscle cells*. They arrive at the place of instability in the lining and line up next to each other. They then begin to produce fibrin and collagen, which are the bricks and mortar needed to build a wall of protection against the unstable plaque.

In some cases, smooth muscle cells are able to form a cap over the plaque, and the danger of an explosion diminishes. Eventually the situation stabilizes and the immediate danger passes. Often this area becomes completely secure, no longer in danger of causing an emergency. Sometimes the scar that the smooth cells formed blocks the artery. If this happens, when we use these muscles more, such as in exercising, the tissue downstream from this area may become starved for oxygen, causing us to experience some pain called angina. If this plaque buildup occurs in the blood vessels in the legs, it is called *peripheral vascular disease.* The pain will pass with time if the stress is reduced.

In other cases, the troops are not able to stabilize the area in time. Despite their efforts, the macrophages and the smooth muscle cells cannot overcome the inflammation and irritation in the artery lining. As a result, the wall containing the plaque rips open, and the blood is suddenly exposed to the fatty gel. At this moment, the blood cells take action and immediately form a blood clot over the area. If the person is taking aspirin regularly, the blood clot formed will be less voracious, large, and "sticky." However, if the person uses tobacco, the clot will be thicker and more likely to block the whole artery, causing major problems.

As plaque grows, it increases the likelihood of it breaking open and spilling its toxic, fatty gel into the blood. The body sends smooth muscle cells to the inflamed area to build a protective wall of fibrin and collagen. If fibrin and collagen can form a cap or scar over the area effectively, the risk of the exploding plaque will diminish. If not, a blood clot will likely form.

IDENTIFYING THE **SYMPTOMS OF A RUPTURED ARTERY**

For many, if not most, of the people who experience the rupture just described, it happens unexpectedly. Most of them are going about their normal, daily business and suddenly become aware of a change in their body. It may start off as a small tickle or irritation. It may feel like tightness in the chest. Or the pain may hit them suddenly, like a baseball bat slamming against their upper body. Other symptoms that may be felt include nausea, sweating, or shortness of breath. In medical school we were taught that any pain between the chin and the belly button is a heart attack until proven otherwise. I dread this day for the many people I care for who are at increased risk of plaque formation.

If the blood vessel experiencing this trauma is in the brain, a *stroke* occurs. If it is in a small non-vital vessel, there may be no sign of a problem at all. If the rupture occurs in a stomach vessel, a severe stomachache may accompany it. If it takes place in the legs, leg cramps usually follow, or one or two toes may turn black or purple. If the rupture occurs closer to the carotid artery in the neck, the effects may be devastating, resulting in paralysis of a part to half of the body. If plaque explodes in the heart, a *heart attack* occurs—a tragic event that takes place every thirty seconds in America, as it did in my mentor friend who went for a jog and never returned.

Exploding plaque in a blood vessel in the brain leads to a stroke. Exploding plaque in the heart leads to a heart attack.

A GLIMPSE OF **WHAT HAPPENS IN THOSE FINAL MOMENTS**

Depending on which part of the blood vessel the plaque is when it ruptures, the final moments may be brief. If it is near the origin of the left main artery of the heart (the beginning of the blood vessel), the heart muscle will die quickly. Blood flow will then cease, and the brain will usually stop functioning, causing the person to lose consciousness within three minutes. If the blockage takes place further downstream in a smaller blood vessel of the heart, less of the heart muscle will be affected and the level of pain will vary.

The victim may only have time to yell out for help. Many times the person never fully knows what happened. In fact, 63 percent of women and 50 percent of men who die of a heart attack *never experienced chest pain prior to their fatal heart attack.*

I often wonder what people think when the reality of the situation hits them. I doubt that they think, *Oops, I shouldn't have eaten all those Big Macs and fries*, or *Gosh, I wish I had exercised more*. More than likely, they immediately think of their loved ones and experience an overwhelming sense of despair as they realize that they may not be able to see them again.

I have sat with lung cancer patients as they sobbed hysterically, asking rhetorically over and over, "Why couldn't I quit? Why couldn't I quit?" As a doctor, in that moment I have felt horrible, inadequate and angry that I couldn't have said or done something to prevent the situation. Unfortunately, at that point all I know to do for them is to comfort them and pray with them.

Ironically, 63 percent of women and 50 percent of men who die of a heart attack never experienced chest pain prior to their fatal heart attack.

IT IS POSSIBLE TO **SURVIVE EXPLODING PLAQUE**

Of those who survive a heart attack, about half will be able to return to their normal activities. They will probably be able to think clearly and experience good quality of life. The other half will be disabled for life to some degree. The range of the disability will be mild shortness of breath to severe heart failure or angina (chest pain with exertion), but their lives will never be the same.

The prospects are not as good for the 635,000[9] that survive a stroke each year. Like heart attacks, many stroke victims die at the time of their first stroke—most of them never having had any previous symptoms.

The best way to understand this event (the process of watching plaque explode) is to go to **www.thesevennumbers.com** and watch the video.

---

9 American Heart Association, "*Heart Disease and Stroke Statistics, 2009 Update*," p. 15.

Watching it unfold will help you understand it and connect the role of each component in the process that we have discussed.

Of those who survive a heart attack, about half will be able to return to their normal activities. The other half will be disabled for life to some degree.

THERE ARE OTHER **CASUALTIES OF THE WAR WITHIN**

In many cases, those who suffer most from the effects of exploding plaque are the loved ones left behind. Even if the heart attack or stroke victim survives, their spouse often has to endure seeing the one they love reduced to an invalid, and their lives are transformed into the role of a caregiver day after day. During the season of life when many couples expect to be traveling and seeing the world, the spouse often finds him or herself trapped by an illness their partner has. Although the spouse may have warned their partner of their poor choices, they had little, if any, power to prevent them. Consequently, dreams go unfulfilled and hopelessness often begins to take over their lives.

Victims also have children who become casualties of the war within. If a parent dies young, his or her kids will miss out on the love, wisdom and support that could have been provided. A daughter may miss being given away on her wedding day by her father. Grandkids may never experience the love and attention that only a grandmother can give. And on it goes. Indeed, our choices don't just affect us—they affect all those our life touches.

There is an excellent bestselling book called *Unexpected Legacy of Divorce: A 25 Year Landmark Study* by Judith S. Wallerstein, Julia M. Lewis, and Sandra Blakeslee. It shows some of the far-reaching effects of broken relationships. If someone wrote a book titled *The Unexpected Legacy of Premature*

Spousal or Parental Death, I wonder what it would say. Yes, I believe the person who dies with a strong faith in God goes to a better place, but what is the effect on their families that are left behind? I think we can be sure to say that they are profoundly affected. Possibly they can turn the loss into positive motivation to live a healthy and vital life themselves. But having a deep emotional scar that one has to get over is challenging. I know that everyone is going to die one day, but as a medical doctor with over twenty-five years of experience, I can confidently say that too many people are dying before their time. This is what I am passionate to see changed.

In many cases, those who suffer most from the effects of exploding plaque are the loved ones left behind. Spouses and children of victims become casualties of the war within. Possibly they can turn the loss into motivation to live a healthy and vital life themselves. But having a deep emotional scar that one has to get over is challenging.

DON'T WAIT UNTIL YOU'RE IN TROUBLE— **GET TESTED NOW!**

The best way to determine if your arteries contain plaque is to get tested. The science of medicine has come very far in its research and treatment of plaque formation. There are tests you can take to reveal if you are at risk of exploding plaque. Here are a few that I would encourage you to consider.

The hsCRP Test

In Number 5, *Blood Pressure*, we discussed how VCAMs and ICAMs act as "red flags" to call for help when the lining becomes inflamed. As it turns out, there is a test we can have done that measures the amount of irritation, or inflammation, in blood vessels, and it tells us if the process of plaque buildup is occurring in our body. It is called the **hsCRP test**. It is able to detect very low levels of inflammation. Consequently, if the level of inflammation is consistently elevated, we know that the walls of the arteries are a smoldering battleground. Excess energy is floating around in the bloodstream with no place to go.

If this is occurring, work must be done to lower the first six numbers. One side note I want to add: When we get sick with a cold or experience other conditions, like rheumatoid arthritis, the hsCRP test will turn up positive for reasons other than plaque buildup. Your doctor can help you interpret the results accurately.

Additionally, research has shown that if your hsCRP is elevated and you take an 81 mg aspirin every day (a baby ASA is enough), then the risk of having a stroke or heart attack is reduced significantly.

The best way to determine if your arteries contain plaque is to get tested. The science of medicine has come very far in its research and treatment of plaque formation. There are tests you can take to reveal if you are at risk of exploding plaque.

The Ultrasound Test

Up until now, everything we have talked about has been from the perspective of the outside looking in. We have discussed the importance of getting our seven numbers and determining what is going on in our blood vessels and heart. Now we are going to change our perspective and look at the blood vessels themselves.

One of the most common methods of looking inside the body is called an **ultrasound**. This test is used to view a baby's growth inside his mother's womb, but it is also used to observe the condition of blood vessels. Any vessels that are not obscured by bones can be looked at with an ultrasound.

This includes the *femoral* arteries of the legs, the aorta in the abdominal area, and the *carotid* arteries of the neck. We can look straight at the artery to see if plaque has begun to accumulate.

The CIMT (Carotid Intimal Medial Thickness) Test

The carotid arteries in particular have become an area of increased study lately because of their strategic location in the neck. When exploding plaque occurs in this area, it can be particularly damaging due to its close proximity to the brain. Consequently, another test has been developed for the carotids. It is called the **CIMT test**.

This CIMT test provides a high resolution examination of the carotid arteries. It is a more sensitive test and thus has been proven to be particularly effective in diagnosing and following plaque buildup in the body.[10] Depending on where you live, a doctor in your area may have access to this test. It's one you may want to consider having performed. You can learn more about it by going to **www.thesevennumbers.com**.

The Heartogram™ or Coronary Calcium Score Test

The last test I want to mention is by far my favorite. It is called the **Heartogram**™ or **Coronary Calcium Score Test**. I believe using this test has been a real lifesaver to my patients. It reveals the calcium buildup inside the coronary arteries. If you look at the figure below, you will see the progression of plaque buildup in an artery. Notice the circular figures at the bottom of the graph. What is shown here in the wall of the artery is the buildup of plaque, which can be of two consistencies: the soft plaque (shown in grey) and the hard plaque (shown in white).

As the process progresses, there is a growing amount of white within the section of growing plaque. This is plaque that has been *calcified*. This hardening takes place as early, soft plaque that has been deposited into the blood vessel wall matures and becomes more stable. Ironically, calcified plaque is less dangerous than soft plaque as it is less likely to rupture. However, it is believed that in untreated instances, where there is hard, calcified plaque, there is also soft plaque looming nearby. While soft plaque is more likely to explode, both work to injure the function and often block the blood vessel.

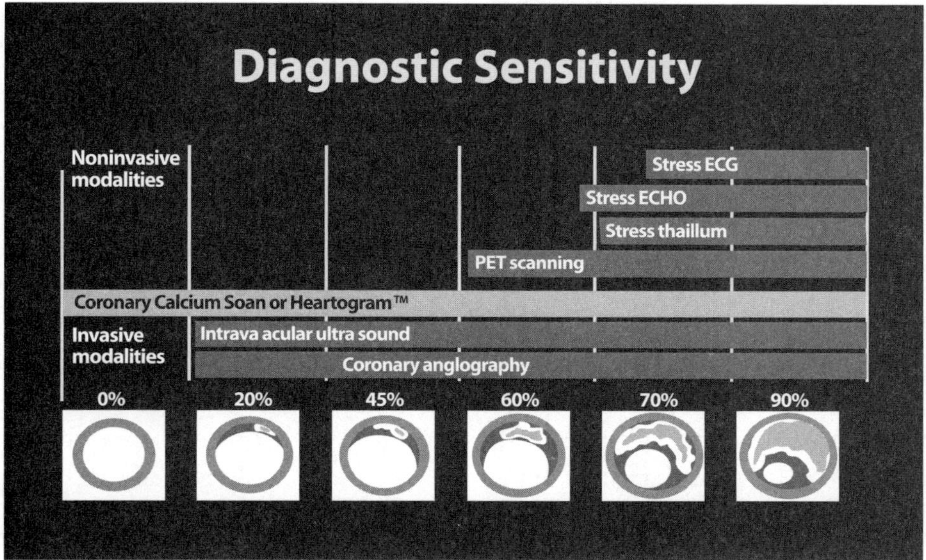

THERE IS **HOPE FOR YOU!**

As I shared earlier, when I was thirty-six years old, I awoke one morning and discovered an obese middle-aged man staring back at me in the mirror. Somehow I managed to be oblivious to the dramatic changes happening during the 15 years when I went from 179 to 242 pounds. I guess I was too busy studying, going through residency and starting a medical practice. I really don't know how a person could overlook the fact they were gaining over 60 pounds, but I did.

Perhaps the most sobering and frightening realization I experienced happened when I turned 40. I had been getting Heartogram™ every couple of years before then, when suddenly, my scan came back positive. It showed

11 Modified from Erbel. *Herz*. 1996;21:75-77

a calcified buildup of plaque in some of my coronary arteries. *Holy cow!* I thought. *I have heart disease!* It was an early detection, but it was there. What could I do?

It was in the midst of understanding this process within my own body and learning what I had to do to slow down or reverse what was happening that I came up with *The Seven Numbers That Will Save Your Life!* Only in this case, it was *my* life I was trying to save. I carefully thought through the process of what was going on inside my arteries. I tried to understand how I ended up with heart disease. In time, answers surfaced.

Remember, this was four years after I had figured out that I was obese. My weight was down 50 pounds to the mid 190s. However, I believe the major reason for my development of heart disease was that I was not exercising consistently. Consequently, I still had a BMI of 28 (ideal is 25 or less), and my good HDL cholesterol was 34, which is low. It's important to note that a low HDL level is the number one symptom in men under the age of 50 who have heart attacks. In any case, my overall HDL/total cholesterol ratio was 4.5, which was definitely higher than it should be. Thankfully, this was my only real abnormality. My blood pressure and blood sugar, which had previously been high when I had a BMI of 34, were back down to normal.

REMEMBER THOSE HEALTHY NUMBERS!

A Healthy BMI is less than 25

A Healthy LDL level is less than 70

A Healthy HDL level is greater than 50 in men and greater than 60 in women

A Healthy HDL/TC Ratio is less than 3.5

In any event, it was time to go to work. The first thing I did to get my HDL up was to start taking vitamin B3, niacin. Initially, I started with 500 mg at bedtime and gradually increased this amount to 1000 mg without too much flushing (a non-dangerous, but uncomfortable side effect of niacin). Soon my HDL was up 20 percent—from 34 to a whopping 40. And my LDL was down below 100. Although my HDL still needed to increase and my LDL decrease, I was moving in the right direction.

At the same time, I decided to cut out starchy carbohydrates like white bread, white rice, non-whole-grain pasta, white potatoes, and corn products. Next, I started to work out every morning at 5:30 a.m. with my cardiologist, Dr. John Osborne. He agreed to train with me to encourage and support me on my journey. I focused on weight lifting with a slow "relaxation" phase of the exercises. This is the portion of the exercise that leads to the most tissue breakdown, and thus, generates the greatest increase in HDL cholesterol.

One year later I had another Heartogram™, and guess what? *The plaque in my arteries was gone!* It had been re-absorbed. The HDL cholesterol had gone in and removed all the plaque. The aging process of my arteries had not only been stabilized but also reversed. The science worked, just as expected. That was in 2000. Since that time I have seen the process of stabilizing and removing plaque from the arteries repeated again and again in a number of people. One note: The soft plaque, which is the more dangerous problem, can always be reabsorbed. In some individuals, we are not able to get the calcified, stable plaque to be removed. Thankfully, I caught my hard plaque before it was too late.

My father took a Heartogram™ and had a relatively high calcium score. To confirm the findings, he had a Computer Tomography Arteriogram (CTA) done on his coronary arteries. It revealed a 40 percent blockage in one of his major heart vessels. Immediately, we went to work with his doctor to get his Seven Numbers under control. One year later, the 40 percent blockage was down to a 20 percent obstruction! How fantastic! We have come so far in understanding how this process occurs that we know how to reverse it! If there is hope for me and hope for my father, there is hope for you!

Figure 2 a Coronary Calcium Scan or Heartogram™. The white is the calcified plaque in the study.

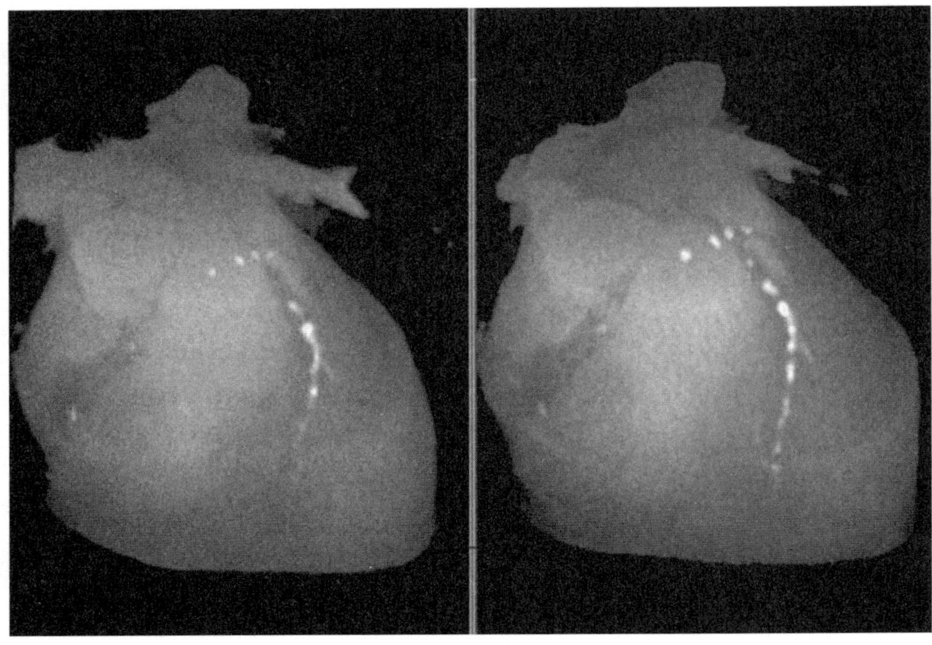

Figure Next. The Computer Tomography Angiogram (CTA) Scan

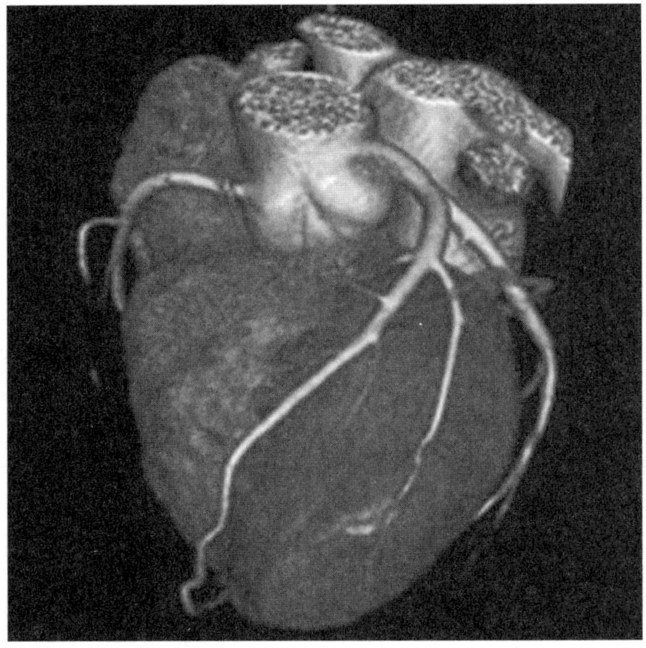

IT'S YOUR TURN TO **SEIZE THE DAY!**

Right now a window of opportunity is open before you. You have a window through knowledge to find out what is going on inside your body—to see if you are at risk of developing exploding plaque, *before* it devastates or ends your life. God has provided you with the wisdom to act before you ever experience the first chest pain. Time and again, it has been proven that when people exercise and eat right, they reduce the risk of diseases caused by exploding plaque.

If you want to lose weight, I wrote a book called *Weight Loss the Jabez Way*. It is based upon an Old Testament passage found in 1 Chronicles 4:10 in which Jabez cries out to God and asks for great blessing and success. He promises to follow the guidance God gives him, and then he concludes his prayer by asking, "…that You would keep me from evil, that I may not cause pain!" (NKJV). *Keep me from evil*—I love this line. Applied to the context of plaque in your arteries, this is like saying, "Keep me from developing a heart attack and stroke, that I may not cause pain to those in my life." At the time this prayer was written, there were not Heartogram™, cholesterol or blood sugar tests, or blood pressure readings. Now there are, and we will be "blessed indeed" if we heed this wisdom to get tested. As God granted Jabez's request, may He also grant ours.

The Nurse's Health Study is a perfect example of what happens when people hear and heed the wisdom to exercise and eat right. Dr. Hu and his colleagues followed over 25,000 female nurses and monitored their lifestyle choices. They published their findings in a recent New England Journal of Medicine article. The women who kept their BMI under 25, exercised regularly, ate a healthy diet of whole-grain products and fresh fruits and vegetables, did not smoke, and only drank alcohol in moderation, decreased their heart attack rate by 88 percent!

As I said at the opening of the book, changes in your body are the result of a logical series of steps. By discovering these changes, you discover the quality of your health and where you are in the process. In many cases, disease can be slowed or even prevented once discovered. The key is to develop "the ears to hear and the eyes to see" what is occurring. With these newly refined senses, you can seize the day and take control of your health. Are you ready?

EXPLODING PLAQUE: PRESSING TOWARD THE GOAL

RECOMMENDED TESTS	UNHEALTHY	INTERMEDIATE	ACHIEVING EXCELLENCE
Heartogram™/Calcium Score	Greater than 100	0-100	0
hsCRP	Greater than 2.0	1.8-2.0	Less than 1.8

PLAYING THE GAME OF HEALTH

5 STEPS TO AVOIDING EXPLODING PLAQUE

AWARENESS: Do you know if you have a problem with exploding plaque? Have you ever had any of the symptoms described earlier? Have you or a member of your family ever had a heart attack or stroke? Make an appointment with your doctor and schedule one of the recommended tests to see what is going on inside your blood vessels.

UNDERSTANDING: Can you see the life-or-death urgency connected with this dangerous condition? Do you understand how the problem of plaque begins and how to begin to eliminate it?

HABITS: What habits in your life are adding to the presence of exploding plaque? How can you eliminate these? Who are you in relationship with that indirectly or directly influences you to make unhealthy food and lifestyle choices?

ACCOUNTABILITY: Who are you in relationship with that encourages you to take care of yourself and live healthy? Who makes you feel that you have value and purpose? Make an effort to connect with these people on a regular basis and be accountable to them with your progress. They are of great value.

SHARING: As you make progress and eliminate plaque from your arteries, journal your journey. You will undoubtedly cross paths with others who are searching for direction and answers, and you will have something to share with them.

CONCLUSION
SOME FINAL FOOD FOR THOUGHT

As we wrap things up, I want to address a question I get asked quite often: "Dr. Conard, is this food *good* or is it *bad*?" Unless you are eating toxins, I believe there is no such thing as "good" or "bad" food. The context of what and how much you are eating is the key. Depending on where you are in life and what is going on inside your body, foods are either more or less likely to help you achieve health.

For instance, there are thin people who eat ice cream and cookies regularly, and because of the exercise they get and the other food they are eating—very healthy food—their body can tolerate these foods without damage. On the other hand, there are obese people who eat a small bowl of strawberries and cream, but their bodies are so fragile, barely hanging on by a thread to their health, that this can push them over the edge into a metabolic firestorm.

Focus on your body and where you are with your health and what you are committed to achieve. Learn The Seven Numbers for your body. Where are you? How in- or out-of-balance are your numbers? Once you know this, then you can gauge what regular consumption of high-caloric foods, like ice cream and cookies, is doing inside your body. Focus on what you want to achieve in your life, what you are committed to. This includes your level of fitness, the frequency at which you eat foods that support or bless your body with lots of vitamins and minerals and fiber, and your energy balance—calories eaten and calories burned. These are the things that determine your success or failure over the long run.

Now you may be wondering, *Dr. Conard, do you eat cookies, cakes, candies, pies, ice cream, fried foods, grilled foods, beef, chips, and pizza?* The answer is yes...but not all at one time, of course. I have actually had people follow me into stores or walk by my table during dinner, just to see what I was eating. I've even had an announcer tell everyone to turn and observe the contents of my plate! But I've never felt ashamed. I love food and I love variety. When I go to Rome, you will find me eating pasta and cheese.

Sometimes I *eat to live*, and other times I *live to eat*. Here's the key: When I know I'm going to eat a high calorie meal, I accommodate and plan for it. I don't like to go to bed at night knowing that my cells are battling back and forth as fat settles in my tissues. So, I plan accordingly. I've done this so many times that my back-up plan for eating a high-calorie meal has become second nature. I would recommend that you do the same thing.

Here is quick cheat sheet that you can follow when you are planning your meals:

If you are **Living to Eat**, you may be eating foods that *increase* your likelihood of having a war occur in your bloodstream while you sleep (metabolic stress in your body). These include…

High-caloric foods
Foods with possible carcinogens, such as fire-broiled or grilled meats
Foods high in fat, especially saturated and trans fatty acids
Foods high in refined sugar or starch
Foods high in sodium

If you are **Eating to Live**, you are eating foods that *decrease* your likelihood of having metabolic stress in your body. These include…

Foods with a lot of vitamins and minerals. Vegetables have many colors because of their nutrients. My wife and I challenge our children to eat a vegetable from each color of the rainbow each day. This makes eating vegetables fun and it gives those who are most precious to me the daily benefits of many different vitamins.

Foods with a lot of fiber. The average American gets 12 to 18 grams of fiber per day. The recommendation is 25 to 30 grams per day. Fiber is what cleans the inside of our digestive system and moves the toxin-producing, bacteria-laden stool out of our body. In addition, if you eat your fiber early in your meal, it tends to decrease the stress the next portion of the meal places on your body.

Foods with lean protein. Protein "sticks to our bones" and keeps us feeling full for several hours. Lean protein contains a lot of good B vitamins and other valuable nutrients. Women especially need to work on eating more lean protein.

Foods with monounsaturated fats that contain DHA and EPA. Monounsaturated fats raise the level of good HDL cholesterol and lower the level of destructive LDL cholesterol in your blood. DHA and EPA are fats from fish. They improve the functioning of our arteries and prevent further destruction. They also reduce inflammation and promote joint health.

As a rule, I recommend you **Eat to Live**. Eat foods that *decrease* the likelihood of creating a crisis inside your body. At the same time, don't be afraid to occasionally eat foods that fall in the **Live to Eat** category. Again, it's about balance, not deprivation.

WHAT IS **THE MOST IMPORTANT MESSAGE YOU CAN TAKE FROM THIS BOOK**?

Given the fact that the everyday choices we make in our lives, our lifestyle choices, determine what happens to us for the next four to eight hours and either gets us into or out of TROUBLE, we have a significant amount of influence over our health.

Be proactive—live the life YOU want to live. Don't sit around in fear, waiting for death or disease to strike. Being proactive about your health and wellness is the foundation of adding years to your life and life to your years.

The most important message you can take from this book is YOU HAVE THE POWER to **manage the risk factors of plaque growth**. It is always easier to "keep the cat in the bag, rather than chase it around to try to get it back in." In other words, it is easier to prevent a problem rather than try to get rid of it. The whole modern practice of preventive medicine stands on this principle. As the old saying goes, "An ounce of prevention is worth a pound of cure."

OKAY, SO **WHERE DO YOU GO FROM HERE**?

We have certainly covered a lot of territory on this journey. Let's take a moment and recap ***The Seven Numbers That Will Save Your Life!*** to keep them fresh in our minds. Remember, these are seven primary areas of importance connected with our body's health and they form the word TROUBLE.

T is ***Training*** – it shows your fitness, based on the amount of activity in your life.
R is ***Roundness*** – it reveals your Body Mass Index (BMI)—weight in relation to height.
O is ***Oil*** – it measures the quantity/quality of fat in your blood (triglycerides, LDL, HDL).
U is ***Unacceptable Sugar*** – it indicates the "sugar stress" levels in your blood.
B is ***Blood Pressure*** – it measures the pressure on the inside of your blood vessels.
L is ***Lousy Habits*** – it identifies behaviors that hold you back from good health.
E is ***Exploding Plaque*** – it exposes the fat buildup inside your arteries that leads to heart attacks and strokes, the #1 killer in the U.S. for both women and men.

By assessing your TROUBLE numbers, you can accurately determine where you are in the spectrum of good health—unhealthy, borderline, or healthy. Now, here's the question:

Where do you fall in this spectrum?

Are you at risk of developing exploding plaque? Are you confident that things are fine when really they are not? The truth is no one is beyond the debilitating grip of cardiovascular disease. All are at risk—from the thinnest to the most obese. I have witnessed too many horrible, pointless heart attacks and strokes to remain silent.

I urge you to find out your numbers. Take an honest look at them and see if you are at risk. If you are in danger in certain areas, begin to make the necessary changes and then recheck those numbers to see how your body is responding. With Roundness (weight), Blood Sugar and/or Blood Pressure, you may want to recheck it daily. With Oil (cholesterol), you may recheck it every three months. And with Exploding Plaque, consider taking the hsCRP test every three months, or the calcium score once every year if you are trying to get it down (or every five years if it is 0). Regularly re-assessing your numbers is a vital part of the process. Don't wait for the government, your friends, or anybody else to take you by the hand and make changes for you. Take the initiative! Find out your numbers. Get in the Game!

Let us know how you are doing on your journey and how we can help. You can shoot me an e-mail at **www.thesevennumbers.com**. If I can educate, equip, or encourage you, I would be honored. To take the next step in your quest for better living, check out the sequel to this book, *The Seven Healers*, at **www.mysevenhealers.com**. Stay in your commitment to living healthy, and may God bless you and your family.

Scott Conard, MD

SECTION THREE
EMPOWERING RESOURCES

Calories Used per Hour in Common Physical Activities

Moderate Physical Activity	Approximate Calories/30 Minutes for a 154 lb Person[1]	Approximate Calories/Hr for a 154 lb Person[1]
Hiking	185	370
Light gardening/yard work	165	330
Dancing	165	330
Golf (walking and carrying clubs)	165	330
Bicycling (<10 mph)	145	290
Walking (3.5 mph)	140	280
Weight lifting (general light workout)	110	220
Stretching	90	180
Moderate Physical Activity	**Approximate Calories/30 Minutes for a 154 lb Person[1]**	**Approximate Calories/Hr for a 154 lb Person[1]**
Running/jogging (5 mph)	295	590
Bicycling (>10 mph)	295	590
Swimming (slow freestyle laps)	255	510
Aerobics	240	480
Walking (4.5 mph)	230	460
Heavy yard work (chopping wood)	220	440
Weight lifting (vigorous effort)	220	440
Basketball (vigorous)	220	440

1 Calories burned per hour will be higher for persons who weigh more than 154 lbs (70 kg) and lower for persons who weigh less. | Source: Adapted from Dietary Guidelines for Americans 2005, page 16, Table 4.
Source: http://www.cdc.gov/healthyweight/physical_activity/index.html

STOP TROUBLES ASSESSMENT

CONGRATULATIONS ON TAKING AN IMPORTANT STEP TOWARDS BETTER HEALTH.

Please take a few minutes to answer the following series of questions to the best of your abilities. After collecting your information go to www.the-sevennumbers.com to enter the information online. Upon completion you will immediately receive a personalized report. After receiving the report you will then be given options for enrolling and learning more.

On the Comprehensive Assessment there are a number of questions that ask for 1 – 10 rating. For these questions use this scale: 1 = Never, 3 = Sometimes, 5 = 50/50, 7 = Mostly, 10 = Always. Don't think too much about your answer. Research has shown that if you go with your first impression your answer is more accurate than if you spend time trying to figure it out.

STOP

QUICK ASSESSMENT:

[ ] My shots are up to date **(see below for names and indications)**
[ ] My tests are up to date **(see below for names and indications)**
[ ] I take natural supplements and vitamins
[ ] I do not take medicine
[ ] I **take** medicine as prescribed **by my doctor**

The last time I had a **full** physical exam was: Month _____ Year ________

Shots

Flu	Month	Year
Tetanus	Month	Year
Pneumonia	Month	Year

Shingles	Month	Year
Varicella	Month	Year
HPV	Month	Year

Tests

Sodium, Potassium, BUN and Creatinine	Month	Year
Kidney function	Month	Year
Liver function	Month	Year
U/A	Month	Year
TSH	Month	Year
Vitamin D level	Month	Year
Bone Density	Month	Year

Physical Exam

The last time I saw my doctor	Month	Year
The last full physical exam with my doctor	Month	Year

[ ] **I would like these results sent to my doctor**

Physician's Name	Fax	Phone

What does your inheritance include

Have your blood relatives, whether they are still alive or not, ever been diagnosed with the following:

[ ] **I don't know my family history**

[ ] Yes [ ] No [ ] I don't know	**Heart disease** Father or brother age 55, or mother or sister before age 65
[ ] Yes [ ] No [ ] I don't know	**Diabetes** Mother, father, sister, brother, son or daughter at any age
[ ] Yes [ ] No [ ] I don't know	**Stroke** Mother, father, sister, brother, son or daughter at any age
[ ] Yes [ ] No [ ] I don't know	**Colon or rectal cancer** Mother, father, sister, brother, son or daughter at any age
[ ] Yes [ ] No [ ] I don't know	**Prostate cancer** Father or brother at any age

[ ] Yes [ ] No [ ] I don't know	**Breast cancer** Mother or sister at any age
[ ] Yes [ ] No [ ] I don't know	**Lung cancer** Father or Mother at any age

TRAINING

Life is meant to be fun and active! Our bodies thrive with "playing." Going from sitting at work and home to putting 20 or 30 minutes of walking or playing (moving around) can cut your risk of heart attacks or strokes in half. It also helps you lose weight, relieve stress, reduce blood pressure and the risk for diabetes and osteoporosis.

QUICK ASSESSMENT:

On average, how many times per week do you engage in physical activity <u>of at least 20 minutes</u>?

[ ] 1 or less
[ ] 2-4
[ ] 5 or more

What is your current excercise level?

[ ] Low
[ ] Moderate
[ ] High

COMPREHENSIVE ASSESSMENT:

Minutes of exercise per week	min
Average number of steps per day (using a pedometer)	steps

1-10	I am active and play for at least 150 minutes per week or over 10,000 steps/day.
1-10	I incorporate resistance training (core training, callisthenic or weights) in my program
1-10	I incorporate aerobic activity (running, swiming, biking, skating, dancing, circuit training, active work or play) into my exercise program.
1-10	I incorporate flexibility exercises (pilates, yoga, stretching) into my exercise program.

ROUNDNESS

Are you overweight or obese? These conditions will shorten, or decrease how long and how well you live. Obesity is linked to just about every health problem, including cancer, heart disease, strokes and diabetes. The best way to avoid or treat obesity is to maintain good eating habits, watch out how much you eat, and "play" as much as possible.

QUICK ASSESSMENT – calculating your Body Mass Index (BMI):

Height:	In Inches	In Centimeters
Weight:	In Pounds	In Kilograms

COMPREHENSIVE ASSESSMENT:

Waist	In Inches	In Centimeters
Neck Circumference	In Inches	In Centimeters
Body Fat	%	

1-10	I monitor and manage the quantity of food I eat (like the Hand Signals of Health), especially when eating out!.
1-10	I eat balanced meals and snacks (lean protein, healthy carbohydrates and fats).

OIL = Lipids

How much fat do you have floating in your blood? Is it healthy fat (HDL) or lethal fat (LDL)? Is there extra energy (triglycerides) present in your blood? Energy you take in (food) when it comes from saturate or trans fat increase the lethal fats; monounsaturated fats and burning energy (exercise) use the triglycerides and elevate the HDL.

QUICK ASSESSMENT:

[ ] I do not know what my cholesterol, triglycerides or HDL are
[ ] My cholesterol, triglycerides and HDL are within normal limits
[ ] I am being treated for an abnormal LDL, HDL, or triglycerides
[ ] I take fish oil (omega 3) supplements every day

COMPREHENSIVE ASSESSMENT:

Cholesterol	mg/dl	Month	Year
Triglycerides	mg/dl	Month	Year
LDL-C	mg/dl	Month	Year
HDL-C	mg/dl	Month	Year
VAP		Month	
Liposcience		Month	
Berkley		Month	

- Servings of red meat per week ______

1-10	I am a success in reducing saturated fat (e.g. whole milk, fried foods, processed foods and fatty meats), trans fats (processed foods), refined carbohydrates (made from white flour and sugar), and high fructose corn syrup (prepackaged food) – read the labels!!.
1-10	I successfully add monounsaturated fats (nuts, avocado, + olive products) and deep water fish (or fish oil supplements) to my diet.

UNACCEPTABLE SUGAR

Sugar (glucose) in your blood is vital for good health. Taking in foods with high levels of sugar causes extra stress inside the body. Weight gain, high blood pressure, diabetes, heart attacks or strokes, and other diseases soon begin to appear in your body. Over 5 – 15 years this will lead to diabetes. Discovering this problem inside your body and taking action can prevent this from occurring! The longer you wait the harder it is to stop or reverse!

QUICK ASSESSMENT:

[ ] My blood sugar is always normal
[ ] My blood sugar before a meal is sometimes between 100-125 or 2 hours after a meal between 140 and 180.
[ ] I have diabetes
[ ] I do not know my blood sugar

COMPREHENSIVE ASSESSMENT:

I eat a rainbow of vegetables and fruits at the first part of my meals each day.	**1-10**

Glucose	mg/dl	**Albumin**	mg/dl	**C peptide**	mg/dl
PreDx Score	1 - 10	**Insulin**	mg/dl	**Hb A1C**	mg/dl

BLOOD PRESSURE

When your heart pumps it leads to more pressure in the arteries, when it relaxes the pressure is lowest. How hard your heart has to work to move the blood and how strong your heart is determines how long and how well your heart lasts. Eating salt (sodium), gaining weight, and not exercising are three ways to make this worse. Over time this leads to heart and kidney failure, strokes, eye damage and heart attacks. Keeping the blood pressure under control makes a big difference in your health! The way you eat and exercise, the weight you maintain, and the supplements and medicine you take can make a big difference to you.

QUICK ASSESSMENT:

[ ] My blood pressure is always normal
[ ] My blood pressure is sometimes greater than 140/90
[ ] I take medicine for high blood pressure
[ ] I do not know my blood pressure

COMPREHENSIVE ASSESSMENT:

I add salt (sodium) to my food	**y/n**
I read labels and try to keep the sodium (Na) under 2000 mg/day	

Blood pressure	mm Hg	Mm Hg	**Heart rate**	bpm

LOUSY HABITS

Lousy habits drive and worsen, or improve and lessen, many health problems. Our hearts and brains are especially susceptible to cigarette smoking or chewing tobacco, excess alcoholic consumption, poor eating habits, not drinking enough water and poor sleep habits. Correcting these will increase the quality and length of your life!

QUICK ASSESSMENT:

[ ] I have more than 2 glasses of wine, beers, or ounces of hard alcohol per day
[ ] I currently smoke cigarettes or chew tobacco
[ ] I get less than 54 hours of sleep per week

COMPREHENSIVE ASSESSMENT:

Do you currently consume alcohol?
[ ] **Yes**
[ ] **No**

12 oz beer	
5 oz wine	
1 oz liquor	

Do you currently use tobacco?
[ ] **Yes**
[ ] **No**

Packs/day	
Chews/day	

	I sleep at least 54 hours each week.
	I am consistent with the time of night that I go to sleep and/or the time of morning that I wake up.
	I reach my water-drinking goal every day (enough water to make my "water" clear or light yellow).
	I substitute water for sugared and/or caffeinated beverages.

EXPLODING PLAQUE AND CELLS

Heart attacks and strokes occur when a plaque containing cholesterol breaks open. Age, high lipids, high sugars, sleep deprivation, weight gain, high blood pressure and/or tobacco have drive the buildup of plaque – lowering or eliminating these slow the process. Cancer occurs when cells in the body begin to grow out of control. Our immune system tries to monitor and prevent this from happening. Many of the same things that lead to plaque build up lead to increased risk of cancer.

QUICK ASSESSMENT: I have been diagnosed with the following

[ ] Heart disease
[ ] Cancer
[ ] Lung disease

COMPREHENSIVE ASSESSMENT: Have you had

[ ] **Heart attack**
[ ] **Heart surgery**
[ ] **Angioplasty or stent**
[ ] **Stroke**
[ ] **Emphysema**
[ ] **Heart failure**
[ ] **Mitral or aortic valve disease or heart murmur**
[ ] **Other cardiovascular disease**
[ ] **Enlarged heart**
[ ] **Atrial fibrillation**
[ ] **Lung cancer**
[ ] **Colon or rectal cancer**
[ ] **Prostrate cancer**

PSA	Month	Year
Colonoscopy	Month	Year
Mammogram	Month	Year
Pap Smear	Month	Year
Hs CRP	Month	Year
Lp PLA	Month	Year
CTA	Month	Year
Calcium score	Month	Year

STRESS AND EMOTIONS

Stress makes a big difference in the choices you make. How much we eat, exercise, take care of your self and how well your immune system and other body systems operate are directly affected. This increases or decreases the quality of your life. Recognizing and treating stress can be very challenging – often it changes slowly so you fail to notice it getting worse. Addressing and managing it improves relationships and the fun you have.

1-10	I am aware of my body and take deep breathes to manage my stress.
1-10	I put aside time to practice deep breathing exercises (the relaxation response, progressive relaxation, or meditation).

1-10	I spend time with friends who call me to be my best and encourage me in my life.
1-10	I give without expectation to the people with whom I come in contact.
1-10	I forgive myself and others for things that don't go well.

1-10	I am living a life of freedom and peace.
1-10	I am grateful for all that I have been given in life.
1-10	I am managing the things I control, encouraging those I influence, and trusting things will work out with the things I don't control.

STOP TROUBLES Assessment *brought to you by The Game of Health (GOH)*™

Name: Patrick Dunn **Date:** 8/8/2010 **Gender:** Male **Age:** 47 yrs **Physician:** Scott Conard, MD

	Your	Goals
S	Up to date	Goal met
T	TSH: Not done	Goal not met
O P	Last Physical: 1/1/1980	Goal not met
T	45 min exercise/week	
R	BMI: 29.8	<25
O U	Chol: 180 Trig 150 LDL 81 HDL 44 Glucose 89	<200 <150 <100 >40 <100
B	144/88	<140/90
L E	Using Tobacco Sleeping 49 h/week PSA: Not done	Goal not met
S	PSA: Not done	Goal met

Personal History

High blood pressure
Low HDL
Family History of prostate cancer

Supplements or Medications

Altace 10 mg/day
Aspirin
Fish oil

Your Risks

	Heart	Stroke	Diabetes	Colon Cancer	Prostate Cancer
5 year risk of disease onset	2.97%	1.56	2.25%	0.28%	0.4%
Your achievable risk	1.12%	0.6%	0.9%	0.16%	0.23%
Difference you can make in your life!!	75%!	75%!	72%!	50%!	33%!

Recommendations

You are due for a PSA
You are due for a physical exam
You are over weight and should consider losing 5-10% of your body weight
Your HDL- cholesterol is not at goal consider playing the HDL game on GOH
Your blood pressure is not at goal
You do not get enough physical activity
Consider starting LDL lowering therapy
Get in the Game of Health! (go to www.gameofhealth.com and sign up)
Taking this assessment has earned you 50 points in the Game of Health!!

HAND SIGNALS OF HEALTH

Palm of Hand	**appropriate portion of lean/low-fat MEAT. It should be no thicker than a deck of cards.**
Width of Fingers	**appropriate portion of CARBOHYDRATES, such as bread, pasta, potatoes, corn and rice. It should be no thicker than a deck of cards.**
Vegetables	**except for starchy ones like potatoes and corn, these are free food. Fill your plate, but avoid high-fat sauces, butter, oils, etc.**

FOR DESSERT

A **SLIVER**	**of pie or cake, no thicker than the width of your finger = about 1 mile or 2,000 steps**
A **SLICE**	**of dessert, about the width of two fingers = 2 miles or 4,000 steps**
A **PIECE**	**of dessert, about the width of three fingers = 3 miles or 6,000 steps**

Extra calories should equal extra Training or exercise. If not, they equal extra weight.

ABOUT SCOTT CONARD, MD

Scott E. Conard, MD, DABFM, FAAFP, has more than twenty years of successful clinical practice, research, medical communications and leadership experience. The truth is that "Dr. Scott" as he was called on his radio show, loves to be a part of people's lives as they grow more vital and successful with their health and wellbeing. His life is dedicated to working with healthcare providers, corporations and individuals to add years to their life and life to their years by empowering them to take control of their health.

Currently he is the Chief Medical Officer of ACAP Health (www.acaphealth.com) and Holmes Murphy & Associates (www.holmesmurphy.com) where he works with corporations, the public sector, and healthcare providers to create systems of Accountable Care (AC) and Accountable Patients (AP) that ensure high value (= safety + quality/cost) for all employee. He passionately believes that physicians must become effective partners with those paying for care to develop new systems that are easy, convenient, and affordable to the employee (and employer). By working together he believes that healthcare providers and employers, in partnership with other key stakeholders, will discover new prescriptions that heal our healthcare system and allow America to maintain a leadership role in the world economy. But that does not mean that he has left direct patient care.

After graduating from the University of South Florida Medical School, he did his residency at a Southwestern Medical School affiliated residency program in family practice at St Paul Hospital. He then moved to Irving Texas where has been in family practice for over 23 years. From 1989 – 2005, his medical practice, called TienaHealth, grew to include 12 medical providers in two locations, with five affiliated sleep laboratories, a durable medical equipment, medical management and research companies. In 2006 Dr Conard merged these programs with Medical Edge Healthcare Group, PA and became the Chief Medical and Strategy Officer for a group of over 500 providers in 20 specialties with practice in Texas, Nevada and North Carolina. In this capacity he worked with a group of highly educated dedicated clinicians caring for over 1 million patients. In 2011 when Medical Edge was sold to Texas Health Resources and Dr Conard left he has began his medical practice again as the founder and leader of GOH (Game of Health) Medical (www.gohmedical.com) serving patients and corporations with innovative, affordable, patient-centric, convenient proactive care in the Dallas Fort Worth Metroplex.

Dr. Conard has been active on the Board of the North Texas Chapter of the American Diabetes Association (ADA). He is the 2012 President of the North Texas Chapter and on the 2012 ADA National Committee on Prevention. He is a diplomat of the American Board of Family Practice and a Fellow of the American Academy of Family Medicine. In the past he received board certification in Bariatric (weight loss) Medicine, additional certification in Behavioral Sleep Medicine and Diabetes Education (as a Certified Diabetic Educator). He has remained active in teaching as an Associate Clinical Professor at University of Texas Southwestern Medical School Department of Family Practice and Community Medicine for 21 years after graduating from the program.

He has been principle investigator in over fifty phase 2, 3, and 4 clinical research trials on pharmacologic agents and therapeutic devices in areas such as obesity, cardiovascular (heart attack and stroke research), infectious disease, diabetes, hypertension, and other health conditions. He is a strong believer in evidence based medicine and medical research. He has been on the study design and writing committee on a number of studies resulting in numerous publications, presentations, and is the author of four books on health and wellbeing.

An international teacher, lecturer and speaker, Dr. Conard has been active in his church teaching *Weight Loss the Jabez Way*, and in the mission's field participating in trips to Mozambique, Rwanda, Honduras, Mexico, Haiti and Guatemala over the last 10 years (www.rapha7ven.org). He has presented over 550 programs to the medical and lay community, and is also involved in writing and publishing numerous scientific articles and health columns. Finally, he has hosted a weekly television talk show (Health Connection), a weekly radio show "All About Life Radio" and has appeared regularly on health related radio and television news programs.